Ballads of Romance

Popular Ballads of the Olden Times

First Series

Frank Sidgwick

Alpha Editions

This edition published in 2024

ISBN : 9789366383811

Design and Setting By
Alpha Editions
www.alphaedis.com
Email - info@alphaedis.com

As per information held with us this book is in Public Domain.
This book is a reproduction of an important historical work. Alpha Editions uses the best technology to reproduce historical work in the same manner it was first published to preserve its original nature. Any marks or number seen are left intentionally to preserve its true form.

PREFACE

OF making selections of ballads there is no end. As a subject for the editor, they seem to be only less popular than Shakespeare, and every year sees a fresh output. But of late there has sprung up a custom of confusing the old with the new, the genuine with the imitation; and the products of civilised days, 'ballads' by courtesy or convention, are set beside the rugged and hard-featured aborigines of the tribe, just as the delicate bust of Clytie in the British Museum has for next neighbour the rude and bold 'Unknown Barbarian Captive.' To contrast by such enforced juxtaposition a ballad of the golden world with a ballad by Mr. Kipling is unfair to either, each being excellent in its way; and the collocation of *Edward* or *Lord Randal* with a ballad of Rossetti's is only of interest or value as exhibiting the perennial charm of the *refrain*.

There exist, however, in our tongue—though x not only in our tongue—narratives in rhyme which have been handed down in oral tradition from father to son for so many ages, that all record of their authorship has long been lost. These are commonly called the Old Ballads. Being traditional, each ballad may exist in more than one form; in most cases the original story is clothed in several different forms. The present series is designed to include all the best of these ballads which are still extant in England and Scotland: Ireland and Wales possess a similar class of popular literature, but each in its own tongue. It is therefore necessary, in issuing this the first volume of the series, to say somewhat as to the methods employed in editing and selecting.

Ballad editors of yore were confronted with perhaps two, perhaps twenty, versions of each ballad; some unintelligibly fragmentary, some intelligibly complete; some in print, some in manuscript, some, perchance, in their own memories. Collating these, they subjected the text to minute revision, omitting and adding, altering and inserting, to suit their personal tastes and standards, literary or polite; and having thus made it over, forgot to record the act, and saw no reason to apologise therefor.

Pioneers like Thomas Percy, Bishop of Dromore, xi and Sir Walter Scott, may well be excused the general censure. The former, living in and pandering to an age which invented and applied those delightful literary adjectives 'elegant' and 'ingenious,' may be pardoned with the more sincerity if one recalls the influence exercised on English letters by his publication. The latter, who played the part of Percy in the matter of Scottish ballads, and was nourished from his boyhood on the *Reliques*, printed for the first time many ballads which still are the best of their class, and was gifted with consummate skill and taste. Both, moreover, did their work scientifically, according to their lights; and both have left at least some of their originals behind them. There is, perhaps, one more exception to the general condemnation. Of William Allingham's *Ballad Book*, as truly a *vade mecum* as Palgrave's lyrical anthology in the same 'Golden Treasury' series, I would speak, perhaps only for sentimental reasons, always with respect, admiring the results of his editing while looking askance at the method, for he mixed his ingredients and left no recipe.

But in the majority of cases there is no obvious excuse for this 'omnium gatherum' process. The self-imposed function of most ballad editors appears to have been the compilation xii of *rifacimenti* in accordance with their private ideas of what a ballad should be. And that such a state of things was permissible is doubtless an indication of the then prevalent attitude of half-interested tolerance assumed towards these memorials of antiquity.

To-day, however, the ballad editor is confronted with the results of the labours, still unfinished, of a comparatively recent school in literary science. These have lately culminated in *The English and Scottish Popular Ballads*, edited by the late Professor Francis James Child of Harvard University. This work, in five large volumes, issued in ten parts at intervals from 1882 to 1898, and left by the editor at his death complete but for the Introduction—*valde deflendus*—gives in full all known variants of the three hundred and five ballads adjudged by its editor to be genuinely 'popular,' with an essay, prefixed to each ballad, on its history, origin, folklore, etc., and notes, glossary, bibliographies, appendices, etc.; exhibiting as a whole unrivalled special knowledge, great scholarly intuition, and years of patient research, aided by correspondents, students, and transcribers in all parts of the world. Lacking Professor Child's Introduction, we cannot exactly tell what his definition of a 'popular' ballad was, or what qualities in a ballad implied xiii exclusion from his collection—*e.g.* he does not admit *The Children in the Wood*: otherwise one can find in this monumental work the whole history and all the versions of nearly all the ballads.

It will be obvious that Professor Child's academic method is suited rather to the scholar than the general reader. As a rule, one text of each ballad is all that is required, which must therefore be chosen—but by what rules? To the scholar, it usually happens that the most ancient and least handled text is the most interesting; but these are too frequently incomplete and unintelligible. The literary dilettante may prefer tasteful decorations by a Percy or a Scott; doubtless Buchan has some admirers: but the student abhors this painting of the lily.

Therefore I have compromised—always a dangerous practice—and I have sought to give, to the best of my judgement, *that authorised text of each ballad which tells in the best manner the completest form of the story or plot.* I have been forced to make certain exceptions, but for all departures from the above rule I have given reasons which, I trust, will be found to justify the procedure; and in all cases the sources of each text or part of the text are indicated.

I am quite aware that it may fairly be asked: xiv Why not assume the immemorial privilege of a ballad editor, and concoct a text for yourself? Why, when any text of a ballad is, as you admit, merely a representative of parallel and similar traditional versions, should you not compile from those other variants a text which should combine the excellences of each, and give us the cream?

There are several objections to this course. However incompetent, I should not shrink from the labour involved; nor do I entirely approve the growing demand for German minuteness and exactitude in editors. But, firstly, the ballad should be subject to variation only while it is in oral circulation. Secondly, editorial garnishing has been overdone already, and my unwillingness to adopt that method is caused as much by the failure of the majority of editors as by the success of the few. Lastly, *chacun a son goût*; there is a kind of literary selfishness in emending and patching to suit one's private taste, and, if any one wishes to do so, he will be most pleased with the result if he does it for himself.

This lengthy *apologia* is necessitated by a departure from the usual custom of ballad-editing. For the rest, my indebtedness to the work of Professor Child will be obvious throughout. Many of his most interesting texts were xv printed for the first time from manuscripts in private hands. These I have not sought to collate, which would, indeed, insult his accuracy and care. But in the case of texts from the Percy Folio, where the labour is rather to decipher than to transcribe accurately, I have resorted not only to the reprint of Hales and Furnivall, but to the Folio itself. The whimsical spelling of this MS. pleases me as often as it irritates, and I have ventured in certain ballads, *e.g. Glasgerion*, to modernise it, and in others, *e.g. Old Robin of Portingale*, to retain it *literatim*: in either case I have reduced to uniformity the orthography of the proper names. Transcripts from other MSS. are reproduced as they stand.

In the general Introduction I have tried to sketch the genesis and history of the ballad impartially in its several aspects, not for scholars and connoisseurs, but for those ready to learn. To supply deficiencies, I have added a list of books useful to the student of English ballads—to go no further afield. Each ballad also is prefaced with an introduction setting forth, besides the source of the text, as succinctly as is consistent with accuracy, the derivation, when known, of the story; the plot of similar foreign ballads; and points of interest in folklore, history, or criticism attached to the particular xvi ballad. Where the story is fragmentary, I have added an argument. It will be realised that such introductions at the best are but a thousandth part of what might be written; but if they shall play the part of *hors d'œuvres*, and whet the appetite to proceed to more solid food, the labour will not be lost.

Difficulties in the text are explained in footnotes. Few things are more vexatious to a reader than constant reference to a glossary; but as compensation for the educational value thus lost, the footnotes are, to a certain extent, progressive; that is to say, a word already explained in a foregoing ballad is not always explained again; and to the best of my ability I have freed the notes from the grotesque blunders observable in most modern editions of ballads.

Besides my indebtedness to the books mentioned in the bibliographical list, I have to acknowledge my thanks to the Rev. Sabine Baring Gould, for permission to use his version of *The Brown Girl*; to Mr. E. K. Chambers, for kindly reading the general Introduction; and to my friend and partner Mr. A. H. Bullen, for constant suggestions and assistance.

F. S.

INTRODUCTION

'Y-a-t-il donc, dans les contes populaires, quelque chose d'intéressant pour un esprit sérieux?'—COSQUIN.

THE old ballads of England and Scotland are fine wine in cobwebbed bottles; and many have made the error of paying too much attention to the cobwebs and not enough attention to the wine. This error is as blameworthy as its converse: we must take the inside and the outside together.

I. WHAT IS A BALLAD?

The earliest sense of the word 'ballad,' or rather of its French and Provençal predecessors, *balada, balade* (derived from the late Latin *ballare*, to dance), was 'a song intended as the accompaniment to a dance,' a sense long obsolete.1 Next came the meaning, a simple song of sentiment or romance, of two verses or more, each of which is sung to the same air, the accompaniment being xviii subordinate to the melody. This sense we still use in our 'ballad-concerts.' Another meaning was that of simply a popular song or ditty of the day, lyrical or narrative, of the kind often printed as a broadsheet. Lyrical *or* narrative, because the Elizabethans appear not to distinguish the two. Read, for instance, the well-known scene in *The Winter's Tale* (Act IV. Sc. 4); here we have both the lyrical ballad, as sung by Dorcas and Mopsa, in which Autolycus bears his part 'because it is his occupation'; and also the 'ballad in print,' which Mopsa says she loves—'for then we are sure it is true.' Immediately after, however, we discover that the 'ballad in print' is the broadside, the narrative ballad, sung of a usurer's wife brought to bed of twenty money-bags at a burden, or of a fish that appeared upon the coast on Wednesday the fourscore of April: in short, as *Martin Marsixtus* says (1592), 'scarce a cat can look out of a gutter but out starts a halfpenny chronicler, and presently a proper new ballet of a strange sight is indited.' Chief amongst these 'halfpenny chroniclers' were William Elderton, of whom Camden records that he 'did arm himself with ale (as old father Ennius did with wine) when he ballated,' and thereby obtained a red nose almost as celebrated as his verses; Thomas Deloney, 'the ballating silkweaver of Norwich'; and Richard Johnson, maker of Garlands. Thus to Milton, to Addison, and even to Johnson, 'ballad' essentially implies singing; but from about the middle of the xix eighteenth century the modern interpretation of the word began to come into general use.

In 1783, in one of his letters, the poet Cowper says: 'The ballad is a species of poetry, I believe, peculiar to this country.... Simplicity and ease are its proper characteristics.' Here we have one of the earliest attempts to define the modern meaning of a 'ballad.' Centuries of use and misuse of the word have left us no unequivocal name for the ballad, and we are forced to qualify it with epithets. 'Traditional' might be deemed sufficient; but 'popular' or 'communal' is more definite. Here we adopt the word used by Professor Child—'popular.'

What, then, do we intend to signify by the expression 'popular ballads'? Far the most important point is to maintain an antithesis between the poetry of the people and the consciously artistic poetry of the schools. Wilhelm Grimm, the less didactic of the two famous brothers, said that the ballad says nothing unnecessary or unreal, and despises external adornment. Ferdinand Wolf, the great critic of the Homeric question, said the ballad must be naïve, objective, not sentimental, lively and erratic in its narrative, without ornamentation, yet with much picturesque vigour.

It is even more necessary to define sharply the line between poetry *of* the people and poetry *for* the people.2 The latter may still be written; xx the making of the former is a lost art. Poetry of the people is either lyric or narrative. This difference is roughly that between song and ballad. 'With us,' says Ritson, 'songs of sentiment, expression, or even description, are properly termed songs, in contradistinction to mere narrative compositions which we now denominate Ballads.' This definition, of course, is essentially modern; we must still insist on the fact that genuine ballads were sung: 'I sing Musgrove,'3 says Sir Thwack in Davenant's *The Wits*, 'and for the Chevy Chase no lark comes near me.' Lastly, we must emphasise that the accompaniment is predominated by the air to which the words are sung. I have heard the modern comic song described as 'the kind in which you hear the words,' thus differentiating it from the drawing-room song, in which the words are (happily) as a rule less audible than the melody. In the ballad, as sung, the words are most important; but it is of vital importance to remember that the ballads were chanted.

II. POETRY OF THE PEOPLE.

Now what is this 'poetry of the people'? One theory is as follows. Every nation or people in the natural course of its development reaches a stage at which it consists of a homogeneous, compact community, with its sentiments xxi undivided by class-distinctions, so that the whole active body forms what is practically an individual. Begging the question, that poetry can be produced by such a body, this poetry is naturally of a concrete and narrative character, and is previous to the poetry of art.

'Therefore,' says Professor Child, 'while each ballad will be idiosyncratic, it will not be an expression of the personality of individuals, but of a collective sympathy; and the fundamental characteristic of popular ballads is therefore the absence of subjectivity and self-consciousness. Though they do not "write themselves," as Wilhelm Grimm has said—though a man and not a people has composed them, still the author counts for nothing, and it is not by mere accident, but with the best reason, that they have come down to us anonymous.'

By stating this, the dictum of one of the latest and most erudite of ballad-scholars, so early in our argument, we anticipate a century or more of criticism and counter-criticism, during which the giants of literature ranged themselves in two parties, and instituted a battle-royal which even now is not quite finished. It will be most convenient if we denominate the one party as that which holds to the communal or 'nebular' theory of authorship, and the other as the anti-communal or 'artistic' theory. The tenet of the former party has already been set forth, namely, that the poetry of the people is a natural and spontaneous production of a community at that stage xxii of its existence when it is for all practical purposes an individual. The theory of the 'artistic' school is that the ballads and folk-songs are the productions of skalds, minstrels, bards, troubadours, or other vagrant professional singers and reciters of various periods; it is allowed, however, that, being subject entirely to oral transmission, these ballads and songs are open to endless variation.

On the Continent, Herder was pioneer, both of the claims of popular poetry and of the nebular theory of authorship. Traditions of chivalry, he says, became poetry in the mouths of the people; but his definition of popular poetry has rather extended bounds. Herder's enthusiasm fired Goethe (who, however, did not wholly accede to the 'nebular' theory) to study the subject, and the effect was soon noticeable in his own poetry. Next came the two great brothers, whose names are ever to be held in honour wherever folklore is studied or folktales read, Jacob and Wilhelm Grimm. Jacob, the more ardent and polemical, insisted on the communal authorship of the poetry of the people; ballad or song 'sings itself.'

Both the Grimms, and especially Jacob, were severely handled by the critic Schlegel, who insisted on the artist. To Schlegel we owe the famous image in which popular poetry is a tower, and the poet an architect. Hundreds may fetch and carry, but all are useless without the direction of the architect. This is specious argument; xxiii but we might reply to Schlegel that an architect is only wanted when the result is required to be an artistic whole. The tower of Babel was built by hundreds of men under no superintendence. Schlegel's intention, however, is no less clear than that of Jacob Grimm, and the two are diametrically opposed.

In England, literary prejudice against the unpolished barbarities and uncouthnesses of the ballad was at no time so pronounced as it was on the Continent, and especially in Germany, during the latter half of the eighteenth century. Indeed, at intervals, the most learned and fantastic critics in England would call attention to the poetry of the people. Sir Philip Sidney's apologetic words are well known:— 'Certainly I must confesse my own barbarousnes, I never heard the olde song of *Percy* and *Duglas*, that I found not my heart mooved more then with a Trumpet.' Addison was bolder. 'It is impossible that anything should be universally tasted and approved by a Multitude, tho' they are only the Rabble of a Nation, which hath not in it some peculiar Aptness to please and gratify the Mind of Man.' With these and other encouragements the popular poetry of England was not lost to sight; and in 1765 the work of the good Bishop of Dromore gave the ballads a place in literature.

Percy's opening remarks, attributing the ballads to the minstrels, are as well known as the scoffs of the hard-hitting Joseph Ritson, who xxiv contemptuously dismissed Percy's theories,4 and refused to believe any ballad to be of earlier origin than the reign of Elizabeth. Sir Walter Scott was quite ready to accept the ballads as the productions of the minstrels, either as 'the occasional effusions of some self-taught bard,' or as abridged from the tales of tradition after the days when, as Alfred de Musset says, 'our old romances spread their wings of gold towards the enchanted world.'

This brings us nearer to our own day. The argument is not closed, although we can discern offers of concession from either side. Svend Grundtvig, editor of the enormous collection of Danish ballads, distinguished the ballad from all forms of artistic literature, and would have the artist left out of sight; Nyrop and the Scandinavian scholars, on the other hand, entirely gave up the notion of communal authorship. Howbeit, the trend of modern criticism,5 on the whole, is towards a common belief regarding most ballads, which may be stated again, in Professor Child's words: 'Though a man and not a people has composed them, still the author counts for nothing, and it is not by mere accident, but with the best reason, that they have come down to us anonymous.'

III. THE GROWTH OF BALLADS.

Let us then picture, however vaguely and uncertainly, the growth of a ballad. It is well known that the folklores of the various races of the world exhibit common features, and that the beliefs, superstitions, tales, even conventionalities of expression, of one race, are found to present constant and remarkable similarities to those of another. Whether these similarities are to be held mere coincidences, or whether they are to be explained by the theory of a common ancestry in the cradle of the world, is a side-issue into which I do not intend to enter. Suffice it that the fact is true, especially of the peoples who speak the Indo-European tongues. The lore which has for its foundation permanent and universal acceptance in the hearts of mankind is preserved by tradition, and remains independent of the criteria applied instinctively and unconsciously to artistic compositions. The community is one at heart, one in mind, one in method of expression. Tales are recited, verses chanted, and the singer of a clan makes his version of a popular story. Simultaneously other singers, it may be of other clans of the same race, or of another race altogether, elaborate their versions of the common theme. Meanwhile the first singer has again recited or chanted his ballad, and, having forgotten the exact wording, has altered it, and perhaps introduced improvements. The same happens in the other cases. xxvi The various audiences carry away as much as they can remember, and recite their versions, again with individual omissions, alterations, and additions. Thus, by ever-widening circles, the tale is distributed in countless forms over an unlimited area. The elements of the story remain, wholly or in part, while the literary clothing is altered according to the 'taste and fancy' of the reciter. The lore is now traditional, whether it be in prose, as Märchen, or in verse, as ballad. And so it remains in oral circulation—and therefore still liable to variation—until it is written down or printed. It is left 'masterless,' unsigned; for of the original author's composition, may be, only a word or two remains. It has passed through many mouths, and has been made over countless times. But once written down it ceases *virûm volitare per ora*; the invention of printing has spoiled the powers of man's memory.

We can now take up the tale at the fifteenth century; let us henceforth confine our attention to England. It is agreed on all sides that the fifteenth century was the period when, in England at least, the ballads first became a prominent feature. Of historical ballads, *The Hunting of the Cheviot* was probably composed as early as 1400 or thereabouts. The romances contemporaneously underwent a change, and took on a form nearer to that of the ballad. Whatever may be the date of the origin of the subject-matter, the literary clothing—language, mode of expression, colour—of no ballad, as we xxvii now have it, is much, earlier than 1400. The only possible exceptions to this statement are one or two of the Robin Hood ballads—attributed to the thirteenth century by Professor Child, but *adhuc sub judice*—and a ballad of sacred legend—*Judas*—which exists in a thirteenth-century manuscript in the library of Trinity College, Cambridge.

During the fifteenth century, the ballads, still purely narrative, were cast abroad through the length and breadth of the land, undergoing continual changes, modifications, enlargements, for better or for worse. They told of romance and chivalry, of historical, quasi-historical, and mythico-historical deeds, of the traditions of the Church and sacred legend, and of the lore that gathers round the most popular of heroes, Robin Hood. The earliest printed English ballad is the *Gest of Robyn Hode*, which now remains in a fragment of about the end of the fifteenth century.

The sixteenth century continued the process of the popularisation of ballads. Minstrels, who, as a class, had been slowly perishing ever since the invention of printing, were now vagrants, and the profession was decadent. Towards the end of the century we hear of Richard Sheale, whom we may describe as the first of the so-called 'Last of the Minstrels.' He describes himself as a minstrel of Tamworth, his business being to chant ballads and tell tales. We know that the ballad of *The Hunting of the Cheviot* was xxviii part of his repertory, for he wrote down his version, which is still preserved in the Ashmolean MSS. At the end of the sixteenth century the minstrels had fallen, in England at least, into entire degradation. In 1597, Percy notes, a statute of Elizabeth was passed including 'minstrels, wandering abroad,' amongst the other 'rogues, vagabonds, and sturdy beggars'; and fifty years later Cromwell made a very similar ordinance.6

In Elizabeth's reign we first meet with the ballad-mongers and professional authors of ballads. Simultaneously, or nearly so, comes the degradation of the word 'ballad,' until it signifies either the genuine popular ballad, or a satirical song, or a broadside, or almost any ditty of the day. Of the ballad-mongers, we have mentioned Elderton, Deloney, and Johnson. We might add a hundred others, from Anthony Munday to Martin Parker, and even Tom Durfey, each of whom contributed largely to the vast mushroom-literature that sprang up and flourished vigorously for the next century. Chappell mentions that seven hundred and ninety-six ballads remained at the end of 1560 in the cupboards of the council-chamber of the Stationers' Company for transference to the new wardens of the succeeding year. These, of course, would consist chiefly of broadsides: the narrations of strange events, monstrosities, or 'true tales' of the day.

xxix It is true that many of the genuine popular ballads were rewritten to suit contemporary taste. But the style of the seventeenth century ballads cannot be compared to the noble straightforwardness and simplicity of the ancient ballad. Let us place side by side the first stanza of the *Hunting of the Cheviot* and the first few verses of *Fair Rosamond*, a very fair specimen of Deloney's work.

The popular ancient ballad wastes no time on preliminaries[7]:—

>'The Persé owt off Northombarlonde
>
>And avowe to God mayd he,
>
>That he wold hunte in the mowntayns

>Off Chyviat within days thre,
>
>In the magger of doughté Dogles;
>
>And all that ever with him be.'

Now for the milk-and-water:—

>'Whenas King Henry rulde this land,
>
>The second of that name,
>
>Besides the queene, he dearly lovde
>
>A faire and comely dame.
>
>Most peerlesse was her beautye founde,
>
>Her favour and her face;
>
>A sweeter creature in this worlde
>
>Could never prince embrace.
>
>Her crisped lockes like threads of golde
>
>Appeard to each man's sight;
>
>Her sparkling eyes, like Orient pearles,
>
>Did cast a heavenly light.'

xxx Ritson's taste actually led him, in comparing the above two first verses, to prefer the latter.

Or again we might contrast *Sir Patrick Spence*—

>'The King sits in Dumferling towne
>
>Drinking the blude reid wine:
>
>"O whar will I get a guid sailor,
>
>To sail this ship of mine?"'

with the *Children in the Wood*:—

>'Now ponder well, you parents deare,
>
>These wordes, which I shall write;
>
>A doleful story you shall heare,
>
>In time brought forth to light.'

Artificial, tedious, didactic. The author of the ancient ballad seldom points, and never draws, a moral, and has unbounded faith in the credulity of the audience. The seventeenth century balladists pitchforked Nature into the midden.

These compositions were printed as soon as written, or, to be exact, they were written for the press. We now class them as broadsides, that is, ballads printed on one side of the paper. The difference between these and the true ballad is the difference between art and nature. The broadside ballad was a form of art, and a low form of art. They were written by hacks for the press, sold in the streets, and pasted on the walls of houses or rooms: Jamieson had a copy of *Young Beichan* which he picked off a wall in Piccadilly. They were generally ornamented with crude woodcuts, remarkable for their artistic shortcomings and infidelity to nature. xxxi Dr. Johnson's well-known lines—though in fact a caricature of Percy's *Hermit of Warkworth*—ingeniously parody their style:—

> 'As with my hat upon my head,
>
> I walk'd along the Strand,
>
> I there did meet another man,
>
> With his hat in his hand.'

Broadside ballads, including a few of the genuine ancient ballads, still enjoy a certain popularity. The once-famous Catnach Press still survives in Seven Dials, and Mr. Such, of Union Street in the Borough, still maintains what is probably the largest stock of broadsides now in existence, including *Lady Isabel and the Elf Knight* (or *May Colvin*), perhaps the most widely dispersed ballad of any.

Minstrels of all sorts were by this time nearly extinct, in person if not in name; their successors were the vendors of broadsides. Nevertheless, survivors of the genuine itinerant reciters of ballads have been discovered at intervals almost to the present day. Sir Walter Scott mentions a person who 'acquired the name of Roswal and Lillian, from singing that romance about the streets of Edinburgh' in 1770 or thereabouts. He further alludes to 'John Graeme, of Sowport in Cumberland, commonly called the Long Quaker, very lately alive.' Ritson mentions a minstrel of Derbyshire, and another from Gloucester, who chanted the ballad of *Lord Thomas and Fair Eleanor*. In 1845 J. H. Dixon wrote of several men he had met, chiefly Yorkshire dalesmen, xxxii not vagrants, but with a local habitation, who at Christmas-tide would sing the old ballads. One of these was Francis King, known then throughout the western dales of Yorkshire, and still remembered, as 'the Skipton Minstrel.' After a merry Christmas meeting, in the year 1844, he walked into the river near Gargrave, in Craven, and was drowned. In Gargrave church-yard lie the remains of perhaps the actual 'last of the minstrels.'[8]

IV. Collectors and Editors.

Now a word or two as to the collectors and editors. To take the broadsides first, the largest collections are at Magdalene College, Cambridge (eighteen hundred broadsides collected by Selden and Pepys), in the Bodleian at Oxford, and in the British Museum. The Bodleian contains collections made by Anthony-à-Wood, Douce, and Rawlinson; the British Museum, the great Roxburghe and Bagford collections, which have been reprinted and edited by William Chappell and the Rev. J. W. Ebsworth for the Ballad Society, as well as other smaller volumes of ballads.

But it is not among the broadsides that our xxxiii noblest ballads are found. The first attempt to collect popular ballads was made by the compiler of three volumes issued in 1723 and 1725. The editor is said to have been Ambrose Phillips, whose name and style combined to produce the word 'namby-pamby.' Next came Allan Ramsay, with 'the *Evergreen*, a collection of Scots poems wrote by the ingenious before 1600.'—'By the ingenious,' we note; not by the 'elegant.' The tide is already beginning to turn; pitchforked Nature will ever come back. Followed the *Tea-Table Miscellany*, also compiled by Allan Ramsay, which contained about twenty popular ballads, the rest being songs and ballads of modern composition. The texts were, of course, chopped about and pruned to suit contemporary taste. It was still necessary to adopt an apologetic attitude on behalf of these barbarous and crude relics of antiquity.

These books paved the way to the great literary triumph of the century. The first edition of Percy's *Reliques* was issued in three volumes, in 1765. He received for it one hundred guineas, instant popularity and patronage, and subsequently, the gratitude of succeeding centuries.

Nevertheless, Percy himself was so far under the influence of his contemporaries that he felt it necessary to adopt the apologetic attitude. In his preface he wrote:— 'In a polished age like the present, I am sensible that many of these reliques of antiquity will require great allowances xxxiv to be made for them.' And again:— 'To atone for the rudeness of the more obsolete poems, each volume concludes with a few modern attempts in the same kind of writing; and to take off from the tediousness of the longer narratives, they are everywhere intermingled with little elegant pieces of the lyrical kind.' In short, he could not trust that large child, the people of England, to take its dose of powder without the conventional treacle. To vary the metaphor, his famous Folio Manuscript he regarded as a Cinderella, and in his capacity as fairy godmother refused to introduce her to the world without hiding the slut's uncouth attire under fine raiment. To which end, besides adding 'little elegant pieces,' he recast and rewrote 'the more obsolete poems,' many of which came direct from the Folio Manuscript. Are we to blame him for yielding to the taste of his day?

He did not satisfy every one. Ritson's immediate outcry is famous—and Ritson stood almost alone. He did, indeed, go so far as to deny the existence of the Folio Manuscript, and Percy was forced to confute him by producing it. In the later editions of the *Reliques*, Percy sought to conciliate him by revising his texts, so as to approximate them more closely to his originals, but still Ritson cried out for the whole truth, and nothing but the truth. And by this time he had supporters. But the whole truth as regards the Folio was not to be divulged yet. The manuscript was most jealously guarded.

xxxv Meanwhile the influence of the publication was having its effect. The poetry of the schools, the poetry of the intellect, the poetry of art, brought to its highest pitch by writers like Dryden and Pope, was shelved; metrically exact diction, artificiality of expression, carefully balanced antitheses, and all the mechanical devices of the school were placed in abeyance. There was a general return to Nature, to simplicity, to straightforwardness—not without imagination, however. Wordsworth, besides insisting, in a famous passage, the Preface to the *Lyrical Ballads*, on the spontaneity of good poetry, recorded his tribute to the *Reliques*: 'I do not think that there is an able writer in verse of the present day who would not be proud to acknowledge his obligation to the *Reliques*.' While failing often to catch the gusto of ancient poetry—witness his translations from Chaucer—Wordsworth was full of the spirit—witness his rifacimento of *The Owl and the Nightingale*—and, best of all, handed it on to Coleridge.9 These two fought side by side against the conventions of the preceding century, against Dryden, Addison, Pope, and last, but not least, Johnson. Some have gone so far as to place the definite turning-point in the year 1798, the year xxxvi of the publication of the *Lyrical Ballads*. Coleridge's *annus mirabilis* was 1797, and the publication of *The Ancient Mariner* is significant of the change. But we need not bind ourselves down to any given year. Enough that the revolution was effected, and that it is scarcely exaggeration to say that it was almost entirely due to the publication of the *Reliques*.

Sir Walter Scott remembered to the day of his death the place where he first made acquaintance with the *Reliques* in his thirteenth year. 'I remember well the spot where I read those volumes for the first time. It was beneath a large platanus-tree, in the ruins of what had been intended for an old-fashioned arbour in the garden I have mentioned. The summer day sped onward so fast, that, notwithstanding the sharp appetite of thirteen, I forgot the hour of dinner, was sought for with anxiety, and was still found entranced in my intellectual banquet.'

Almost immediately competitors appeared in the field, and especial attention was given to Scotland, exceedingly rich ground, as it proved. In 1769, David Herd published his collection of *Ancient and Modern Scots Songs, Heroic Ballads, etc.* Then, at intervals of two or three years only, came the compilations of Evans, Pinkerton, Ritson, Johnson; in 1802 Sir Walter Scott's *Minstrelsy of the Scottish Border*, fit to be placed side by side with the *Reliques*; in 1806 Jamieson's *Popular Ballads and Songs*; then Finlay, Gilchrist, Laing, and Utterson. In 1828 the xxxvii egregious Peter Buchan produced *Ancient Ballads and Songs of the North of Scotland, hitherto unpublished.* Buchan hints that he kept a pedlar or beggarman—'a wight of Homer's craft'— travelling through Scotland to pick up ballads; and one of the two— probably Buchan—must have been possessed of powerful inventive faculties. Each of Buchan's ballads is tediously spun out to enormous and unnecessary length, and is filled with solecisms and inanities quite inconsistent with the spirit of the true ballad. But Buchan undoubtedly gained fresh material, however much he clothed it; and his ballads are now reprinted, as Professor Child says, for much the same reason that thieves are photographed.

Scotland continued the work with two excellent students and pioneers, George Kinloch and William Motherwell. Next, Robert Chambers published a collection of eighty ballads, some being spurious. This was in 1829. Thirty years later Chambers came to the conclusion that 'the high-class romantic ballads of Scotland ... are not older than the early part of the eighteenth century, and are mainly, if not wholly, the production of one mind.' And this one mind, he thinks, was probably that of Elizabeth, Lady Wardlaw, the acknowledged forger of the ballad *Hardyknute*, which deceived so many. Chambers, of course, was absurdly mistaken.

So the work of collecting and editing progressed through the nineteenth century, till it culminated in the final edition of Professor Child's *English xxxviii and Scottish Popular Ballads.* But even this is scarcely his greatest benefaction to the study of ballads. We must confess that had it not been for the insistence of this American scholar, the Percy Folio Manuscript would remain a sealed book. For six years Professor Child persecuted Dr. Furnivall, who persecuted in turn the owners of the Folio, even offering sums of money, for permission to print the MS. Eventually they succeeded, and not only succeeded in giving to the world an exact reprint,10 but also once for all secured the precious original for the British Museum, where it now remains.11

And what is this manuscript? In brief, it is an example of the commonplace books which abounded in the seventeenth century. But it is unique in containing a large proportion of early romances and ballads, as well as the lyrics of the day. Of the hundreds of commonplace books made during that century, no other example is known which contains such matter, for the obvious and simple reason that such matter was despised.12 The handwriting is put by experts at about 1650; it cannot be much later, and one song in it contains a passage which fixes the date of that song xxxix to the year 1643. Percy discovered the book 'lying dirty on the floor under a bureau in the parlour' of his friend Humphrey Pitt of Shifnal, in Shropshire, 'being used by maids to light the fire.' Mr. Pitt's fires were lighted with half-pages torn out from incomparably early and precious versions of certain Robin Hood and other ballads. Percy notes that he was very young when he first got possession of the MS., and had not then learned to reverence it. When he put it into boards to lend to Dr. Johnson, the bookbinder pared the margins, and cut away top and bottom lines. In editing the *Reliques*, Percy actually tore out pages 'to save the trouble of transcribing.' In spite of all, it remains a unique and inestimably valuable manuscript. Its writer was presumably a Lancashire man, from his use of certain dialect words, and was assuredly a man of slight education; nevertheless a national benefactor.

In speaking of manuscripts, we must not omit to mention the Scottish collectors. Most of them went to work in the right way, seeking out aged men and women in out-of-the-way corners of Scotland, and taking down their ballads from their lips. If we condemn these editors for subsequently adorning the traditional versions, we must be grateful to them for preserving their manuscripts so that we can still read the ballads as they received them. The old ladies of Scotland seem to have possessed better memories than the old men. Besides Sir Walter Scott's anonymous 'Old Lady,' there was another to xl whom we owe some of the finest versions of the Scottish ballads. This was Mrs. Brown, daughter of Professor Gordon of Aberdeen. Born in 1747, she learned most of her ballads before she was twelve years old, or before 1759, from the singing of her aunt, Mrs. Farquhar of Braemar. From about twenty to forty years later, she repeated her ballads, first to Jamieson, and afterwards to William Tytler, each of whom compiled a manuscript. The latter, the Tytler-Brown MS., unfortunately is lost, but the ballads are practically all known from the other manuscript and various sources.

Perhaps the richest part of our stock are the Scottish and Border ballads. Beside them, most of our mawkish English ballads look pale and withered. The reason, perhaps, may be traced to the effect of natural surroundings on literature. The English ballads were printed or written down at a period which is early compared with the date of collection of the Scottish ballads. In fact, it is only during the last hundred and thirty years that the ballads of Scotland have been recovered from oral tradition. In mountainous districts, where means of communication and intercourse are naturally limited, tradition dies more hard than in countries where there are no such barriers.

Moreover, as Professor Child points out, 'oral transmission by the unlettered is not to be feared nearly so much as by minstrels, nor by minstrels nearly so much as modern editors.' Svend Grundtvig illustrates this from his xli twenty-nine versions of the Danish ballad 'Ribold and Guldborg.' In versions from recitation, he has shown that there occur certain verses which have never been printed, but which are found in old manuscripts; and these recited versions also contain verses which have never been either printed or written down in Danish, but which are to be found still in recitation, not only in Norwegian and Swedish versions, but even in Icelandic tradition of two hundred years' standing.

Such, then, is the history of our ballads, so far as it may be stated in a few pages. With regard to origins, the 'nebular' theory cannot be summarily dismissed;13 but, after weighing the evidence and arguments, the balance of probability would seem to lie with the supporters of the 'artistic' theory in a modified form. The ballad may say, with Topsy, 'Spec's I growed'; but *vires adquirit eundo* is only true of the ballad to a certain point; progress, which includes the invention of printing and the absorption into cities of the unsophisticated rural population, has since killed the oral circulation of the ballad. Thus it was not an unmixed evil that in the Middle Ages, as a rule, the ballads were neglected; for this neglect, while it rendered the discovery of their sources almost impossible, gave the ballads for a time into the safe-keeping xlii of their natural possessors, the common people. Civilisation, advancing more swiftly in some countries than in others, has left rich stores here, and little there. Our close kinsmen of Denmark, and the rest of Scandinavia, possess a ballad-literature of which they do well to be proud; and Spain is said to have inherited even better legacies. A study of our native ballads yields much interest, much delight, and much regret that the gleaning is comparatively so small. But what we still have is of immense value. The ballads may not be required again to revoke English literature from flights into artificiality and subjectivity; but they form a leaf in the life of the English people, they uphold the dignity of human nature, they carry us away to the legends, the romances, the beliefs, the traditions of our ancestors, and take us out of ourselves to 'fleet the time carelessly, as they did in the golden world.'

BALLADS IN THE FIRST SERIES

THE only possible method of classifying ballads is by their subject-matter; and even thus the lines of demarcation are frequently blurred. It is, however, possible to divide them roughly into several main classes, such as ballads of romance and chivalry; ballads of superstition and of the supernatural; Arthurian, historical, sacred, domestic ballads; ballads of Robin Hood and other outlaws; and so forth.

The present volume is concerned with ballads of romance and chivalry; but it is useless to press too far the appropriateness of this title. *The Nutbrown Maid*, for instance, is not a true ballad at all, but an amœbæan idyll, or dramatic lyric. But, on the whole, these ballads chiefly tell of life, love, death, and human passions, of revenge and murder and heroic deed.

'These things are life:

And life, some think, is worthy of the Muse.'

They are left unexpurgated, as they came down to us: to apologise for things now left unsaid would be to apologise not only for the heroic epoch in which they were born, but also for human nature.

xliv And how full of life that heroic epoch was! Of what stature must Lord William's steed have been, if Lady Maisry could hear him sneeze a mile away! How chivalrous of Gawaine to wed an ugly bride to save his king's promise, and how romantic and delightful to discover her on the morrow to have changed into a well-fared may!

The popular Muse regards not probability. Old Robin, who hails from Portugal, marries the daughter of the mayor of Linne, that unknown town so dear to ballads. In *Young Bekie*, Burd Isbel's heart is wondrous sair to find, on liberating her lover, that the bold rats and mice have eaten his yellow hair. We must not think of objecting that the boldest rat would never eat a live prisoner's hair, but only applaud the picturesque indication of durance vile.

In the same ballad, Burd Isbel, 'to keep her from thinking lang'—a prevalent complaint—is told to take 'twa marys' on her journey. We suddenly realise how little there was to amuse the Burd Isbels of yore. Twa marys provide a week's diversion. Otherwise her only occupation would have been to kemb her golden hair, or perhaps, like Fair Annie, drink wan water to preserve her complexion.

But if their occupations were few, their emotions and affections were strong. Ellen endures insult after insult from Child Waters with the faithful patience of a Griselda. Hector the hound recognises Burd Isbel after years of separation. Was any lord or lady in need of xlv a messenger, there was sure to be a little boy at hand to run their errand soon, faithful unto death. On receipt of painful news, they kicked over the table, and the silver plate flew into the fire. When roused, men murdered with a brown sword, and ladies with a penknife. We are left uncertain whether the Cruel Mother did not also 'howk' a grave for her murdered babe with that implement.

But readers will easily pick out and enjoy for themselves other instances of the naïve and picturesque in these ballads.

GLOSSARY OF BALLAD COMMONPLACES

There survive in ballads a few conventional phrases, some of which appear to have been preserved by tradition beyond an understanding of their import. I give here short notes on a few of the more interesting phrases and words which appear in the present volume, the explanations being too cumbrous for footnotes.

Bow.

'bent his bow and swam,' *Lady Maisry*, 21.²; *Johney Scot*, 10.²; *Lord Ingram and Chiel Wyet*, 12.²; etc.

'set his bent bow to his breast,' *Lady Maisry*, 22.³; *Lord Ingram and Chiel Wyet*, 13.³; *Fause Footrage*, 33.¹; etc.

Child attempts no explanation of this striking phrase, which, I believe, all editors have either openly or silently neglected. Perhaps 'bent' may mean *un*-bent, *i.e.* with the string of the bow slacked. If so, for what reason was it done before swimming? We can understand that it would be of advantage to keep the string dry, but how is it better protected when unstrung? Or, again, was it carried unstrung, xlvii and literally 'bent' before swimming? Or was the bow solid enough to be of support in the water?

Some one of these explanations may satisfy the first phrase (as regards swimming); but why does the messenger 'set his bent bow to his breast' before leaping the castle wall? It seems to me that the two expressions must stand or fall together; therefore the entire lack of suggestions to explain the latter phrase drives me to distrust of any of the explanations given for the former.

A suggestion recently made to me appears to dispose of all difficulties; and, once made, is convincing in its very obviousness. It is, that 'bow' means 'elbow,' or simply 'arm.' The first phrase then exhibits the commonest form of ballad-conventionalities, picturesque redundancy: the parallel phrase is 'he slacked his shoon and ran.' In the second phrase it is, indeed, necessary to suppose the wall to be breast-high; the messenger places one elbow on the wall, pulls himself up, and vaults across.

Lexicographers distinguish between the Old English *bōg* or *bōh* (O.H.G. buog = arm; Sanskrit, bahu-s = arm), which means arm, arch, bough, or bow of a ship; and the Old English *boga* (O.H.G. bogo), which means the archer's bow. The distinction is continued in Middle English, from the twelfth to the fifteenth century. Instances of the use of the word as equivalent to 'arm' may be found in Old English in *King Alfred's Translation of Gregory's Pastoral Care* (E.E.T.S., 1871, ed. H. Sweet) written in West Saxon dialect of the ninth century.

It is true that the word does not survive elsewhere in this meaning, but I give the suggestion for what it is worth.

BRIAR.

'briar and rose,' *Douglas Tragedy*, 18, 19, 20; *Fair Margaret and Sweet William*, 18, 19, 20; *Lord Lovel*, 9, 10; etc.

'briar and birk,' *Lord Thomas and Fair Annet*, 29, 30; *Fair Janet*, 30; etc.

'roses,' *Lady Alice*, 5, 6. (See introductory note to *Lord Lovel*, p. 67.)

The ballads which exhibit this pleasant conception that, after death, the spirits of unfortunate lovers pass into plants, trees, or flowers springing from their graves, are not confined to European folklore. Besides appearing in English, Gaelic, Swedish, Norwegian, Danish, German, French, Roumanian, Romaic, Portuguese, Servian, Wendish, Breton, Italian, Albanian, Russian, etc., we find it occurring in Afghanistan and Persia. As a rule, the branches of the trees intertwine; but in some cases they only bend towards each other, and kiss when the wind blows.

In an Armenian tale a curious addition is made. A young man, separated by her father from his sweetheart because he was of a different religion, perished with her, and the two were buried by their friends in one grave. Roses grew from the grave, and sought to intertwine, but a *thorn-bush* sprang up between them and prevented it. The thorn here is symbolical of religious belief.

PIN.

'thrilled upon a pin,' *Glasgerion*, 10.[2].

'knocked at the ring,' *Fair Margaret and Sweet William*, 11.[2].

(*Cp*. 'lifted up the pin,' *Fair Janet*, 14.[2].)

Throughout the Scottish ballads the expression is 'tirl'd at the pin,' *i.e.* rattled or twisted the pin.

The pin appears to have been the external part of the door-latch, attached by day thereto by means of a leathern thong, which at night was disconnected with the latch to prevent any unbidden guest from entering.

Thus any one 'tirling at the pin' does not attempt to open the door, but signifies his presence to those within.

The ring was merely part of an ordinary knocker, and had nothing to do with the latching of the door.

Sword.

'bright brown sword,' *Glasgerion*, 22.[1]; *Old Robin of Portingale*, 22.[1]; *Child Maurice*, 26.[1], 27.[1]; 'good browne sword,' *Marriage of Sir Gawaine*, 24.[3]; etc.

'dried it on his sleeve,' *Glasgerion*, 22.[2]; *Child Maurice*, 27.[2] ('on the grasse,' 26.[2]); 'straiked it o'er a strae,' *Bonny Birdy*, 15.[2]; 'struck it across the plain,' *Johney Scot*, 32.[2]; etc.

In Anglo-Saxon, the epithet 'brún' as applied to a sword has been held to signify either that the sword was of bronze, or that the sword gleamed. It has further been suggested that sword-blades may have been artificially bronzed, like modern gun-barrels.

'Striped it thro' the straw' and many similar expressions all refer to the whetting of a sword, generally just before using it. Straw (unless 'strae' and 'straw' mean something else) would appear to be very poor stuff on which to sharpen swords, but Glasgerion's sleeve would be even less effective; l perhaps, however, 'dried' should be 'tried.' Johney Scot sharpened his sword on the ground.

Miscellaneous.

'gare' = gore, part of a woman's dress; *Brown Robin*, 10.[4]; cp. *Glasgerion*, 19.[4].

Generally of a knife, apparently on a chatelaine. But in *Lamkin* 12.[2], of a man's dress.

'Linne,' 'Lin,' *Young Bekie*, 5.[4]; *Old Robin of Portingale*, 2.[1].

A stock ballad-locality, castle or town. Perhaps to be identified with the city of Lincoln, perhaps with Lynn, or King's Lynn, in Norfolk, where pilgrims of the fourteenth century visited the Rood Chapel of Our Lady of Lynn, on their way to Walsingham; with equal probability it is not to be identified at all with any known town.

'shot-window,' *Gay Goshawk*, 8.[3]; *Brown Robin*, 3.[3]; *Lamkin*, 7.[3]; etc.

This commonplace phrase seems to vary in meaning. It may be 'a shutter of timber with a few inches of glass above it' (Wodrow's *History of the Sufferings of the Church of Scotland*, Edinburgh, 1721-2, 2 vols., in vol. ii. p. 286); it may be simply 'a window to open and shut,' as Ritson explains it; or again, as is implied in Jamieson's *Etymological Dictionary of the Scottish Language*, an outshot window, or bow-window. The last certainly seems to be intended in certain instances.

'thought lang' *Young Bekie*, 16.[4]; *Brown Adam*, 5.[2]; *Johney Scot*, 6.[2]; *Fause Footrage*, 25.[2]; etc.

This simply means 'thought it long,' or 'thought it slow,' as we should say in modern slang; in short, 'was bored,' or 'weary.'

'wild-wood swine,' a simile for drunkenness, *Brown Robin*, 7.[4]; *Fause Footrage*, 16.[4].

Cp. Shakespeare, *All's Well that Ends Well*, Act IV. 3, 286: 'Drunkenness is his best virtue; for he will be swine-drunk.' It seems to be nothing more than a popular comparison.

NOTE ON THE ILLUSTRATIONS

The illustrations on pp. 28, 75, and 118 are taken from Royal MS. 10. E. iv. (of the fourteenth century) in the British Museum, where they occur on folios 34 *verso*, 215 *recto*, and 254 *recto* respectively. The designs in the original form a decorated margin at the foot of each page, and are outlined in ink and roughly tinted in three or four colours. Much use is made of them in the illustrations to J. J. Jusserand's *English Wayfaring Life in the Middle Ages*, where M. Jusserand rightly points out that this MS. 'has perhaps never been so thoroughly studied as it deserves.'

Footnotes

1. For the subject of the origin of the ballad and its refrain in the *ballatio* of the dancing-ring, see *The Beginnings of Poetry*, by Professor Francis B. Gummere, especially chap. v. The beginning of the whole subject is to be found in the universal and innate practices of accompanying manual or bodily labour by a rhythmic chant or song, and of festal song and dance.

2. See the first essay, 'What is "Popular Poetry"?' in *Ideas of Good and Evil*, by W. B. Yeats (1903), where this distinction is not recognised.

3. *Little Musgrave and Lady Barnard* (see p. 19, etc.).

4. 'The truth really lay between the two, for neither appreciated the wide variety covered by a common name' (*The Mediæval Stage*, E. K. Chambers, 1903). See especially chapters iii. and iv. of this work for an admirably complete and illuminating account of minstrelsy.

5. For the most recent discussions, see Bibliography, p. lii.

6. But these were only re-enactments of existing laws. See Chambers, *Mediæval Stage*, i. p. 54.

7. A good notion of the way in which the old ballads plunge *in medias res* may be obtained by reading the Index of First Lines.

8. Unless we may attribute that distinction to the blind Irish bard Raftery, who flourished sixty years ago. See various accounts of him given by Lady Gregory (*Poets and Dreamers*) and W. B. Yeats (*The Celtic Twilight*, 1902). But he appears to have been more of an improviser than a reciter.

9. 'He [Coleridge] said the *Lyrical Ballads* were an experiment about to be tried by him and Wordsworth, to see how far the public taste would endure poetry written in a more natural and simple style than had hitherto been attempted; totally discarding the artifices of poetical diction, and making use only of such words as had probably been common in the most ordinary language since the days of Henry II.'—*Hazlitt*.

10. *Bishop Percy's Folio Manuscript*, edited by J. W. Hales and F. J. Furnivall, 4 vols., 1867-8. Printed for the Early English Text Society and subscribers.

11. Additional MS. 27, 879.

12. Cp. *Love's Labour's Lost:*—
ARMADO. Is there not a ballad, boy, of the King and the Beggar?
MOTH. The world was very guilty of such a ballad some three ages since; but I think now 'tis not to be found.

13. Professor Gummere (*The Beginnings of Poetry*) is perhaps the strongest champion of this theory, and takes an extreme view.

GLASGERION

> Ther herde I pleyen on an harpe
>
> That souned bothe wel and sharpe,
>
> Orpheus ful craftely,
>
> And on his syde, faste by,
>
> Sat the harper Orion,
>
> And Eacides Chiron,
>
> And other harpers many oon,
>
> And the Bret<u>A</u> Glascurion.
>
> —CHAUCER, *Hous of Fame*, III.

THE TEXT, from the Percy Folio, luckily is complete, saving an omission of two lines. A few obvious corrections have been introduced, and the Folio reading given in a footnote. Percy printed the ballad in the *Reliques*, with far fewer alterations than usual.

THE STORY is also told in a milk-and-water Scotch version, *Glenkindie*, doubtless mishandled by Jamieson, who 'improved' it from two traditional sources. The admirable English ballad gives a striking picture of the horror of 'churlës blood' proper to feudal days.

In the quotation above, Chaucer places Glascurion with Orpheus, Arion, and Chiron, four great harpers. It is not improbable that Glascurion and Glasgerion represent the Welsh bard Glas Keraint (Keraint the Blue Bard, the chief bard wearing a blue robe of office), said to have been an eminent poet, the son of Owain, Prince of Glamorgan.

The oath taken 'by oak and ash and thorn' (stanza 18) is a relic of very early times. An oath 'by corn' is in *Young Hunting*.

<u>A.</u> From Skeat's edition: elsewhere quoted 'gret Glascurion.'

GLASGERION

    1.

    1.4 Folio:— 'where cappe & candle yoode.' Percy in the *Reliques* (1767) printed 'cuppe and *caudle* stoode.'

    1.6 'wood,' mad, wild (with delight).

Glasgerion was a king's own son,
And a harper he was good;
He harped in the king's chamber,
Where cup and candle stood,
And so did he in the queen's chamber,
Till ladies waxed wood.

2.

And then bespake the king's daughter,
And these words thus said she:

. . . . .
. . . . .

3.

3.² 'blin,' cease.

Said, 'Strike on, strike on, Glasgerion,
Of thy striking do not blin;
There's never a stroke comes over this harp
But it glads my heart within.'

4.

4.⁴ *i.e.* durst never speak my mind.

'Fair might you fall, lady,' quoth he;
'Who taught you now to speak?
I have loved you, lady, seven year;
My heart I durst ne'er break.'

5.

'But come to my bower, my Glasgerion,
When all men are at rest;
As I am a lady true of my promise,
Thou shalt be a welcome guest.'

6.

6.[1] 'home'; Folio *whom*.

But home then came Glasgerion,

A glad man, Lord, was he!

'And come thou hither, Jack, my boy,

Come hither unto me.

7.

7.[3,4] These lines are reversed in the Folio.

'For the king's daughter of Normandy

Her love is granted me,

And before the cock have crowen

At her chamber must I be.'

8.

'But come you hither, master,' quoth he,

'Lay your head down on this stone;

For I will waken you, master dear,

Afore it be time to gone.'

9.

9.[1] 'lither,' idle, wicked.

But up then rose that lither lad,

And did on hose and shoon;

A collar he cast upon his neck,

He seemed a gentleman.

10.

10.[2] 'thrilled,' twirled or rattled; cp. 'tirled at the pin,' a stock ballad phrase (Scots).

And when he came to that lady's chamber,

He thrilled upon a pin.

The lady was true of her promise,

Rose up, and let him in.

11.

He did not take the lady gay

To bolster nor no bed,

But down upon her chamber-floor

Full soon he hath her laid.

12.

12.² 'yode,' went.

He did not kiss that lady gay

When he came nor when he yode;

And sore mistrusted that lady gay

He was of some churlës blood.

13.

But home then came that lither lad,

And did off his hose and shoon.

And cast that collar from about his neck;

He was but a churlës son:

'Awaken,' quoth he, 'my master dear,

I hold it time to be gone.

14.

14.⁴ 'time': Folio *times*.

'For I have saddled your horse, master,

Well bridled I have your steed;

Have not I served a good breakfast?

When time comes I have need.'

15.

But up then rose good Glasgerion,

And did on both hose and shoon,

And cast a collar about his neck;

He was a kingës son.

16.

And when he came to that lady's chamber,

He thrilled upon a pin;

The lady was more than true of her promise,

Rose up, and let him in.

17.

17.3 Folio *you are*.

Says, 'Whether have you left with me

Your bracelet or your glove?

Or are you back returned again

To know more of my love?'

18.

Glasgerion swore a full great oath

By oak and ash and thorn,

'Lady, I was never in your chamber

Sith the time that I was born.'

19.

'O then it was your little foot-page

Falsely hath beguiled me':

And then she pull'd forth a little pen-knife

That hanged by her knee,

Says, 'There shall never no churlës blood

Spring within my body.'

20.

But home then went Glasgerion,

A woe man, good [Lord], was he;

Says, 'Come hither, thou Jack, my boy,

Come thou thither to me.

21.

'For if I had killed a man to-night,

Jack, I would tell it thee;

But if I have not killed a man to-night,

Jack, thou hast killed three!'

22.

22.[2] Another commonplace of the ballads. The Scotch variant is generally, 'And striped it thro' the straw.' See special section of the Introduction.

And he pull'd out his bright brown sword,

And dried it on his sleeve,

And he smote off that lither lad's head,

And asked no man no leave.

23.

23.[1,2] 'till,' to, against.

He set the sword's point till his breast,

The pommel till a stone;

Thorough that falseness of that lither lad

These three lives were all gone.

YOUNG BEKIE

THE TEXT is that of the Jamieson-Brown MS., taken down from the recitation of Mrs. Brown about 1783. In printing the ballad, Jamieson collated with the above two other Scottish copies, one in MS., another a stall-copy, a third from recitation in the north of England, a fourth 'picked off an old wall in Piccadilly' by the editor.

THE STORY has several variations of detail in the numerous versions known (Young Bicham, Brechin, Bekie, Beachen, Beichan, Bichen, Lord Beichan, Lord Bateman, Young Bondwell, etc.), but the text here given is one of the most complete and vivid, and contains besides one feature (the 'Belly Blin') lost in all other versions but one.

A similar story is current in the ballad-literature of Scandinavia, Spain, and Italy; but the English tale has undoubtedly been affected by the charming legend of Gilbert Becket, the father of Saint Thomas, who, having been captured by Admiraud, a Saracen prince, and held in durance vile, was freed by Admiraud's daughter, who then followed him to England, knowing no English but 'London' and 'Gilbert'; and after much tribulation, found him and was married to him. 'Becket' is sufficiently near 'Bekie' to prove contamination, but not to prove that the legend is the origin of the ballad.

The Belly Blin (Billie Blin = billie, a man; blin', blind, and so Billie Blin = Blindman's Buff, formerly 7 called Hoodman Blind) occurs in certain other ballads, such as *Cospatrick*, *Willie's Lady*, and the *Knight and the Shepherd's Daughter*; also in a mutilated ballad of the Percy Folio, *King Arthur and King Cornwall*, under the name Burlow Beanie. In the latter case he is described as 'a lodly feend, with seuen heads, and one body,' breathing fire; but in general he is a serviceable household demon. Cp. German *bilwiz*, and Dutch *belewitte*.

YOUNG BEKIE

1.

YOUNG BEKIE was as brave a knight

As ever sail'd the sea;

An' he's doen him to the court of France,

To serve for meat and fee.

2.

He had nae been i' the court of France

A twelvemonth nor sae long,

Til he fell in love with the king's daughter,

An' was thrown in prison strong.

3.

The king he had but ae daughter,

Burd Isbel was her name;

An' she has to the prison-house gane,

To hear the prisoner's mane.

4.

4.¹ 'borrow,' ransom.

'O gin a lady woud borrow me,

At her stirrup-foot I woud rin;

Or gin a widow wad borrow me,

I woud swear to be her son.

5.

'Or gin a virgin woud borrow me,

I woud wed her wi' a ring;

I'd gi' her ha's, I'd gie her bowers,

The bonny tow'rs o' Linne.'

6.

6.¹,² 'but ... ben,' out ... in.

O barefoot, barefoot gaed she but,

An' barefoot came she ben;

It was no for want o' hose an' shoone,

Nor time to put them on;

7.

7.³ 'stown,' stolen.

But a' for fear that her father dear,

Had heard her making din:

She's stown the keys o' the prison-house dor

An' latten the prisoner gang.

8.

8.3 'rottons,' rats.

O whan she saw him, Young Bekie,

Her heart was wondrous sair!

For the mice but an' the bold rottons

Had eaten his yallow hair.

9.

She's gi'en him a shaver for his beard,

A comber till his hair,

Five hunder pound in his pocket,

To spen', and nae to spair.

10.

She's gi'en him a steed was good in need,

An' a saddle o' royal bone,

A leash o' hounds o' ae litter,

An' Hector called one.

11.

Atween this twa a vow was made,

'Twas made full solemnly,

That or three years was come and gane,

Well married they shoud be.

12.

He had nae been in's ain country

A twelvemonth till an end,

Till he's forc'd to marry a duke's daughter,

Or than lose a' his land.

13.

'Ohon, alas!' says Young Bekie,
'I know not what to dee;
For I canno win to Burd Isbel,
And she kensnae to come to me.'

14.

O it fell once upon a day
Burd Isbel fell asleep,
An' up it starts the Belly Blin,
An' stood at her bed-feet.

15.

15.² The MS. reads 'How y you.'

'O waken, waken, Burd Isbel,
How [can] you sleep so soun',
Whan this is Bekie's wedding day,
An' the marriage gain' on?

16.

16.³ 'marys,' maids.

'Ye do ye to your mither's bow'r,
Think neither sin nor shame;
An' ye tak twa o' your mither's marys,
To keep ye frae thinking lang.

17.

'Ye dress yoursel' in the red scarlet,
An' your marys in dainty green,
An' ye pit girdles about your middles
Woud buy an earldome.

18.

'O ye gang down by yon sea-side,
An' down by yon sea-stran';

Sae bonny will the Hollans boats

Come rowin' till your han'.

19.

'Ye set your milk-white foot abord,

Cry, Hail ye, Domine!

An' I shal be the steerer o't,

To row you o'er the sea.'

20.

She's tane her till her mither's bow'r,

Thought neither sin nor shame,

An' she took twa o' her mither's marys,

To keep her frae thinking lang.

21.

She dress'd hersel' i' the red scarlet.

Her marys i' dainty green,

And they pat girdles about their middles

Woud buy an earldome.

22.

An' they gid down by yon sea-side,

An' down by yon sea-stran';

Sae bonny did the Hollan boats

Come rowin' to their han'.

23.

She set her milk-white foot on board,

Cried 'Hail ye, Domine!'

An' the Belly Blin was the steerer o't,

To row her o'er the sea.

24.

Whan she came to Young Bekie's gate,

She heard the music play;

Sae well she kent frae a' she heard,

It was his wedding day.

25.

She's pitten her han' in her pocket,

Gin the porter guineas three;

'Hae, tak ye that, ye proud porter,

Bid the bride-groom speake to me.'

26.

O whan that he cam up the stair,

He fell low down on his knee:

He hail'd the king, an' he hail'd the queen,

An' he hail'd him, Young Bekie.

27.

'O I've been porter at your gates

This thirty years an' three;

But there's three ladies at them now,

Their like I never did see.

28.

'There's ane o' them dress'd in red scarlet,

And twa in dainty green,

An' they hae girdles about their middles

Woud buy an earldome.'

29.

29.[1] 'bierly,' stately.

Then out it spake the bierly bride,

Was a' goud to the chin:

'Gin she be braw without,' she says,

'We's be as braw within.'

30.

Then up it starts him, Young Bekie,

An' the tears was in his ee:

'I'll lay my life it's Burd Isbel,

Come o'er the sea to me.'

31.

O quickly ran he down the stair,

An' whan he saw 'twas she,

He kindly took her in his arms,

And kiss'd her tenderly.

32.

'O hae ye forgotten, Young Bekie

The vow ye made to me,

Whan I took ye out o' the prison strong

Whan ye was condemn'd to die?

33.

'I gae you a steed was good in need,

An' a saddle o' royal bone,

A leash o' hounds o' ae litter,

An' Hector called one.'

34.

It was well kent what the lady said,

That it wasnae a lee,

For at ilka word the lady spake,

The hound fell at her knee.

35.

'Tak hame, tak hame your daughter dear,

A blessing gae her wi',

For I maun marry my Burd Isbel,

That's come o'er the sea to me.'

36.

'Is this the custom o' your house,
Or the fashion o' your lan',
To marry a maid in a May mornin',
An' send her back at even?'

OLD ROBIN OF PORTINGALE

TEXT.— The Percy Folio is the sole authority for this excellent ballad, and the text of the MS. is therefore given here *literatim*, in preference to the copy served up 'with considerable corrections' by Percy in the *Reliques*. I have, however, substituted a few obvious emendations suggested by Professor Child, giving the Folio reading in a footnote.

THE STORY is practically identical with that of *Little Musgrave and Lady Barnard*; but each is so good, though in a different vein, that neither could be excluded.

The last stanza narrates the practice of burning a cross on the flesh of the right shoulder when setting forth to the Holy Land—a practice which obtained only among the very devout or superstitious of the Crusaders. Usually a cross of red cloth attached to the right shoulder of the coat was deemed sufficient.

OLD ROBIN OF PORTINGALE

    1.

GOD! let neuer soe old a man

Marry soe yonge a wiffe

As did old Robin of Portingale!

He may rue all the dayes of his liffe.

    2.

2.[1] 'Lin,' a stock ballad-locality: cp. *Young Bekie*, 5.[4].

Ffor the Maior's daughter of Lin, God wott,

He chose her to his wife,

& thought to haue liued in quiettnesse

With her all the dayes of his liffe.

    3.

They had not in their wed bed laid,

Scarcly were both on sleepe,

But vpp she rose, & forth shee goes

To Sir Gyles, & fast can weepe.

4.

Saies, 'Sleepe you, wake you, faire Sir Gyles

Or be not you within?'

.   .   .   .   .

.   .   .   .   .

5.

5.³ 'vnbethought.' The same expression occurs in two other places in the Percy Folio, each time apparently in the same sense of 'bethought [him] of.'

'But I am waking, sweete,' he said,

'Lady, what is your will?'

'I haue vnbethought me of a wile,

How my wed lord we shall spill.

6.

6.¹,³ 'Four and twenty': the Folio gives '24' in each case.

'Four and twenty knights,' she sayes,

'That dwells about this towne,

Eene four and twenty of my next cozens,

Will helpe to dinge him downe.'

7.

With that beheard his litle foote page,

As he was watering his master's steed,

Soe   .   .   .   .   .

His verry heart did bleed;

8.

8.¹ 'sikt,' sighed. The Folio reads *sist*.

He mourned, sikt, & wept full sore;

I sweare by the holy roode,

The teares he for his master wept

Were blend water & bloude.

- 42 -

9.

With that beheard his deare master

As in his garden sate;

Sayes, 'Euer alacke, my litle page,

What causes thee to weepe?

10.

'Hath any one done to thee wronge,

Any of thy fellowes here?

Or is any of thy good friends dead,

Which makes thee shed such teares?

11.

11.[1], 12.[1] The Folio reads *bookes man*; but see 15.[1]

'Or if it be my head kookes man

Greiued againe he shalbe,

Nor noe man within my howse

Shall doe wrong vnto thee.'

12.

'But it is not your head kookes man,

Nor none of his degree,

But or tomorrow ere it be noone,

You are deemed to die;

13.

'& of that thanke your head steward,

& after your gay ladie.'

'If it be true, my litle foote page,

Ile make thee heyre of all my land.'

14.

14.[2] 'thye,' thrive: the Folio reads *dye*.

'If it be not true, my deare master,

God let me neuer thye.'

'If it be not true, thou litle foot page,

A dead corse shalt thou be.'

15.

He called downe his head kooke's man:

'Cooke, in kitchen super to dresse':

'All & anon, my deare master,

Anon att your request.'

16.

'& call you downe my faire Lady,

This night to supp with mee.'

  . . . . .

  . . . . .

17.

& downe then came that fayre Lady,

Was cladd all in purple & palle,

The rings that were vpon her fingers

Cast light thorrow the hall.

18.

'What is your will, my owne wed Lord,

What is your will with me?'

'I am sicke, fayre Lady,

Sore sicke, & like to dye.'

19.

19.[1] '&' = an, if.

'But & you be sicke, my owne wed Lord,

Soe sore it greiueth mee,

But my 5 maydens & my selfe

Will goe & make your bedd,

20.

20.³ 'next': the Folio reads *first* again; probably the copyist's error.

'& at the wakening of your first sleepe,

You shall haue a hott drinke made,

& at the wakening of your next sleepe

Your sorrowes will haue a slake.'

21.

He put a silke cote on his backe,

Was 13 inches folde,

& put a steele cap vpon his head,

Was gilded with good red gold;

22.

& he layd a bright browne sword by his side

& another att his ffeete,

& full well knew old Robin then

Whether he shold wake or sleepe.

23.

23.⁴ 'ginne,' door-latch.

& about the middle time of the night

Came 24 good knights in,

Sir Gyles he was the formost man,

Soe well he knew that ginne.

24.

24.⁴ 'quicke,' alive. The last word was added by Percy in the Folio.

Old Robin with a bright browne sword

Sir Gyles' head he did winne,

Soe did he all those 24,

Neuer a one went quicke out [agen];

25.

25.[4] Added by Hales and Furnivall.

None but one litle foot page

Crept forth at a window of stone,

& he had 2 armes when he came in

And [when he went out he had none].

26.

26.[1,2] *light* and *bright* are interchanged in the Folio.

Vpp then came that ladie light

With torches burning bright;

Shee thought to haue brought Sir Gyles a drinke,

But shee found her owne wedd knight;

27.

& the first thing that this ladye stumbled vpon,

Was of Sir Gyles his ffoote;

Sayes, 'Euer alacke, & woe is me,

Heere lyes my sweete hart roote!'

28.

& the 2d. thing that this ladie stumbled on,

Was of Sir Gyles his head;

Sayes, 'Euer alacke, & woe is me,

Heere lyes my true loue deade!'

29.

Hee cutt the papps beside her brest,

& bad her wish her will,

& he cutt the eares beside her heade,

& bade her wish on still.

30.

'Mickle is the man's blood I haue spent

To doe thee & me some good';

Sayes, 'Euer alacke, my fayre Lady,

I thinke that I was woode!'

31.

He call'd then vp his litle foote page,

& made him heyre of all his land,

.   .   .   .   .

.   .   .   .   .

32.

32.³ 'went': the Folio gives *sent*.

& he shope the crosse in his right sholder

Of the white flesh & the redd,

& he went him into the holy land,

Wheras Christ was quicke and dead.

LITTLE MUSGRAVE AND LADY BARNARD

THE TEXT here given is the version printed, with very few variations, in *Wit Restor'd*, 1658, *Wit and Drollery*, 1682, Dryden's *Miscellany*, 1716, etc. The Percy Folio contains a fragmentary version, consisting of some dozen stanzas. Child says that all the Scottish versions are late, and probably derived, though taken down from oral tradition, from printed copies. As recompense, we have the Scotch *Bonny Birdy*.

THE STORY would seem to be purely English. That it was popular long before the earliest known text is proved by quotations from it in old plays: as from *Fair Margaret and Sweet William*. Merrythought in *The Knight of the Burning Pestle* (1611) sings from this ballad a version of stanza 14, and Beaumont and Fletcher also put quotations into the mouths of characters in *Bonduca* (circ. 1619) and *Monsieur Thomas* (circ. 1639). Other plays before 1650 also mention it.

The reader should remember, once for all, that burdens are to be repeated in every verse, though printed only in the first.

LITTLE MUSGRAVE AND LADY BARNARD

    1.

As it fell one holy-day,

Hay downe

As many be in the yeare,

When young men and maids together did goe,

Their mattins and masse to heare;

    2.

Little Musgrave came to the church-dore;—

The preist was at private masse;—

But he had more minde of the faire women

Then he had of our lady['s] grace.

    3.

3.² 'pall,' a cloak: some versions read *pale*.

The one of them was clad in green,
Another was clad in pall,
And then came in my lord Barnard's wife,
The fairest amonst them all.

4.

She cast an eye on Little Musgrave,
As bright as the summer sun;
And then bethought this Little Musgrave,
'This lady's heart have I woonn.'

5.

Quoth she, 'I have loved thee, Little Musgrave,
Full long and many a day';
'So have I loved you, fair lady,
Yet never word durst I say.'

6.

6.[2] 'deight,' *i.e.* dight, decked, dressed.

'I have a bower at Bucklesfordbery,
Full daintyly is it deight;
If thou wilt wend thither, thou Little Musgrave,
Thou's lig in mine armes all night.'

7.

Quoth he, 'I thank yee, fair lady,
This kindnes thou showest to me;
But whether it be to my weal or woe,
This night I will lig with thee.'

8.

With that he heard, a little tynë page,
By his ladye's coach as he ran:
'All though I am my ladye's foot-page,

Yet I am Lord Barnard's man.

9.

'My lord Barnard shall knowe of this,

Whether I sink or swim';

And ever where the bridges were broake

He laid him downe to swimme.

10.

'A sleepe or wake, thou Lord Barnard,

As thou art a man of life,

For Little Musgrave is at Bucklesfordbery,

A bed with thy own wedded wife.'

11.

'If this be true, thou little tinny page,

This thing thou tellest to me,

Then all the land in Bucklesfordbery

I freely will give to thee.

12.

'But if it be a ly, thou little tinny page,

This thing thou tellest to me,

On the hyest tree in Bucklesfordbery

Then hanged shalt thou be.'

13.

He called up his merry men all:

'Come saddle me my steed;

This night must I to Bucklesfordbery,

For I never had greater need.'

14.

And some of them whistled, and some of them sung,

And some these words did say,

And ever when my lord Barnard's horn blew,

'Away, Musgrave, away!'

15.

15.¹ 'thresel-cock,' throstle, thrush.

'Methinks I hear the thresel-cock,

Methinks I hear the jaye;

Methinks I hear my Lord Barnard,

And I would I were away!'

16.

'Lye still, lye still, thou little Musgrave,

And huggell me from the cold;

'Tis nothing but a shephard's boy

A driving his sheep to the fold.

17.

'Is not thy hawke upon a perch,

Thy steed eats oats and hay,

And thou a fair lady in thine armes,

And wouldst thou bee away?'

18.

With that my lord Barnard came to the dore,

And lit a stone upon;

He plucked out three silver keys

And he open'd the dores each one.

19.

He lifted up the coverlett,

He lifted up the sheet:

'How now, how now, thou Little Musgrave,

Doest thou find my lady sweet?'

20.

'I find her sweet,' quoth Little Musgrave,

'The more 'tis to my paine;

I would gladly give three hundred pounds

That I were on yonder plaine.'

21.

'Arise, arise, thou Little Musgrave,

And put thy clothës on;

It shall nere be said in my country

I have killed a naked man.

22.

'I have two swords in one scabberd,

Full deere they cost my purse;

And thou shalt have the best of them,

And I will have the worse.'

23.

The first stroke that Little Musgrave stroke,

He hurt Lord Barnard sore;

The next stroke that Lord Barnard stroke,

Little Musgrave nere struck more.

24.

With that bespake this faire lady,

In bed whereas she lay:

'Although thou'rt dead, thou Little Musgrave,

Yet I for thee will pray.

25.

'And wish well to thy soule will I,

So long as I have life;

So will I not for thee, Barnard,

Although I am thy wedded wife.'

26.

He cut her paps from off her brest;

Great pitty it was to see

That some drops of this ladies heart's blood

Ran trickling downe her knee.

27.

27.[4] 'wood,' wild, fierce.

'Woe worth you, woe worth, my mery men all,

You were nere borne for my good;

Why did you not offer to stay my hand,

When you see me wax so wood?

28.

'For I have slaine the bravest sir knight

That ever rode on steed;

So have I done the fairest lady

That over did woman's deed.

29.

'A grave, a grave,' Lord Barnard cry'd,

'To put these lovers in;

But lay my lady on the upper hand,

For she came of the better kin.'

THE BONNY BIRDY

TEXT.—From the Jamieson-Brown MS. Jamieson, in printing this ballad, enlarged and rewrote much of it, making the burden part of the dialogue throughout.

THE STORY is much the same as that of *Little Musgrave and Lady Barnard*; but the ballad as a whole is worthy of comparison with the longer English ballad for the sake of its lyrical setting.

THE BONNY BIRDY

1.

THERE was a knight, in a summer's night,

Was riding o'er the lee, (*diddle*)

An' there he saw a bonny birdy,

Was singing upon a tree. (*diddle*)

O wow for day! (*diddle*)

An' dear gin it were day! (*diddle*)

Gin it were day, an' gin I were away,

For I ha' na lang time to stay. (*diddle*)

2.

2.4 'blate,' astonished, abashed.

'Make hast, make hast, ye gentle knight,

What keeps you here so late?

Gin ye kent what was doing at hame,

I fear you woud look blate.'

3.

'O what needs I toil day an' night,

My fair body to kill,

Whan I hae knights at my comman',

An' ladys at my will?'

4.

'Ye lee, ye lee, ye gentle knight,

Sa loud's I hear you lee;

Your lady's a knight in her arms twa

That she lees far better nor thee.'

5.

'Ye lee, ye lee, you bonny birdy,

How you lee upo' my sweet!

I will tak' out my bonny bow,

An' in troth I will you sheet.'

6.

'But afore ye hae your bow well bent,

An' a' your arrows yare,

I will flee till another tree,

Whare I can better fare.'

7.

7.[1] 'clecked,' hatched.

'O whare was you gotten, and whare was ye clecked?

My bonny birdy, tell me';

'O I was clecked in good green wood,

Intill a holly tree;

A gentleman my nest herryed

An' ga' me to his lady.

8.

8.[1] 'A Farrow Cow is a Cow that gives Milk in the second year after her Calving, having no Calf that year.'—Holme's *Armoury*, 1688.

'Wi' good white bread an' farrow-cow milk

He bade her feed me aft,

An' ga' her a little wee simmer-dale wanny,

To ding me sindle and saft.

9.

8.³ 'wanny,' wand, rod: 'simmer-dale,' apparently = summer-dale.

8.⁴ 'sindle,' seldom.

'Wi' good white bread an' farrow-cow milk

I wot she fed me nought,

But wi' a little wee simmer-dale wanny

She dang me sair an' aft:

Gin she had deen as ye her bade,

I wouldna tell how she has wrought.'

10.

10.⁵ 'crap,' top.

10.⁶ 'dight,' freely, readily.

The knight he rade, and the birdy flew,

The live-lang simmer's night,

Till he came till his lady's bow'r-door,

Then even down he did light:

The birdy sat on the crap of a tree,

An' I wot it sang fu' dight.

11.

'O wow for day! (*diddle*)

An' dear gin it were day! (*diddle*)

Gin it were day, and gin I were away,

For I ha' na lang time to stay.' (*diddle*)

12.

'What needs ye lang for day, (*diddle*)

An' wish that you were away? (*diddle*)

Is no your hounds i' my cellar,

Eating white meal and gray?' (*diddle*)

'O wow for day,' *etc.*

13.

'Is nae you[r] steed in my stable,

Eating good corn an' hay?

An' is nae your hawk i' my perch-tree,

Just perching for his prey?

An' is nae yoursel i' my arms twa?

Then how can ye lang for day?'

14.

'O wow for day! (*diddle*)

An' dear gin it were day! (*diddle*)

For he that's in bed wi' anither man's wife

Has never lang time to stay.' (*diddle*)

15.

15.1-4 Cp. *Clerk Sanders*, 15.

Then out the knight has drawn his sword,

An' straiked it o'er a strae,

An' thro' and thro' the fa'se knight's waste

He gard cauld iron gae:

An' I hope ilk ane sal sae be serv'd

That treats ane honest man sae.

FAIR ANNIE

THE TEXT is that of Scott's *Minstrelsy*, 'chiefly from the recitation of an old woman.' Scott names the ballad 'Lord Thomas and Fair Annie,' adding to the confusion already existing with 'Lord Thomas and Fair Annet.'

THE STORY.—Fair Annie, stolen from the home of her father, the Earl of Wemyss, by 'a knight out o'er the sea,' has borne seven sons to him. He now bids her prepare to welcome home his real bride, and she meekly obeys, suppressing her tears with difficulty. Lord Thomas and his new-come bride hear, through the wall of their bridal chamber, Annie bewailing her lot, and wishing her seven sons had never been born. The bride goes to comfort her, discovers in her a long-lost sister, and departs, thanking heaven she goes a maiden home.

Of this ballad, Herd printed a fragment in 1769, some stanzas being incorporated in the present version. Similar tales abound in the folklore of Scandinavia, Holland, and Germany. But, three hundred years older than any version of the ballad, is the lay of Marie de France, *Le Lai de Freisne*; which, nevertheless, is only another offshoot of some undiscovered common origin.

It is imperative (in 4.4) that Annie should *braid* her hair, as a sign of virginity: married women only bound up their hair, or wore it under a cap.

FAIR ANNIE

    1.

    'IT'S narrow, narrow, make your bed,

    And learn to lie your lane;

    For I'm ga'n o'er the sea, Fair Annie,

    A braw bride to bring hame.

    Wi' her I will get gowd and gear;

    Wi' you I ne'er got nane.

    2.

    'But wha will bake my bridal bread,

    Or brew my bridal ale?

    And wha will welcome my brisk bride,

That I bring o'er the dale?'

3.

'It's I will bake your bridal bread,
And brew your bridal ale;
And I will welcome your brisk bride,
That you bring o'er the dale.'

4.

'But she that welcomes my brisk bride
Maun gang like maiden fair;
She maun lace on her robe sae jimp,
And braid her yellow hair.'

5.

'But how can I gang maiden-like,
When maiden I am nane?
Have I not born seven sons to thee,
And am with child again?'

6.

She's taen her young son in her arms,
Another in her hand,
And she's up to the highest tower,
To see him come to land.

7.

'Come up, come up, my eldest son,
And look o'er yon sea-strand,
And see your father's new-come bride,
Before she come to land.'

8.

'Come down, come down, my mother dear,
Come frae the castle wa'!

I fear, if langer ye stand there,

Ye'll let yoursell down fa'.'

9.

And she gaed down, and farther down,

Her love's ship for to see,

And the topmast and the mainmast

Shone like the silver free.

10.

And she's gane down, and farther down,

The bride's ship to behold,

And the topmast and the mainmast

They shone just like the gold.

11.

She's taen her seven sons in her hand,

I wot she didna fail;

She met Lord Thomas and his bride,

As they came o'er the dale.

12.

'You're welcome to your house, Lord Thomas,

You're welcome to your land;

You're welcome with your fair ladye,

That you lead by the hand.

13.

'You're welcome to your ha's, ladye,

You're welcome to your bowers;

You're welcome to your hame, ladye,

For a' that's here is yours.'

14.

'I thank thee, Annie, I thank thee, Annie,

Sae dearly as I thank thee;

You're the likest to my sister Annie,

That ever I did see.

15.

15.³ 'scoup,' fly, hasten.

'There came a knight out o'er the sea,

And steal'd my sister away;

The shame scoup in his company,

And land where'er he gae!'

16.

She hang ae napkin at the door,

Another in the ha',

And a' to wipe the trickling tears,

Sae fast as they did fa'.

17.

17.⁴ 'had' = haud, hold.

And aye she served the long tables,

With white bread and with wine;

And aye she drank the wan water,

To had her colour fine.

18.

And aye she served the lang tables,

With white bread and with brown;

And ay she turned her round about

Sae fast the tears fell down.

19.

And he's taen down the silk napkin,

Hung on a silver pin,

And aye he wipes the tear trickling

A' down her cheek and chin.

20.

And aye he turned him round about,

And smil'd amang his men;

Says, 'Like ye best the old ladye,

Or her that's new come hame?'

21.

When bells were rung, and mass was sung,

And a' men bound to bed,

Lord Thomas and his new-come bride

To their chamber they were gaed.

22.

22.[1] 'forbye,' apart.

Annie made her bed a little forbye,

To hear what they might say;

'And ever alas,' Fair Annie cried,

'That I should see this day!

23.

'Gin my seven sons were seven young rats

Running on the castle wa',

And I were a gray cat mysell,

I soon would worry them a'.

24.

24.[2] 'lilly lee,' lovely lea.

'Gin my seven sons were seven young hares,

Running o'er yon lilly lee,

And I were a grew hound mysell,

Soon worried they a' should be.'

25.

And wae and sad Fair Annie sat,
And drearie was her sang,
And ever, as she sobb'd and grat,
'Wae to the man that did the wrang!'
26.
'My gown is on,' said the new-come bride,
'My shoes are on my feet,
And I will to Fair Annie's chamber,
And see what gars her greet.
27.
'What ails ye, what ails ye, Fair Annie,
That ye make sic a moan?
Has your wine barrels cast the girds,
Or is your white bread gone?
28.
'O wha was't was your father, Annie,
Or wha was't was your mother?
And had ye ony sister, Annie,
Or had ye ony brother?'
29.
'The Earl of Wemyss was my father,
The Countess of Wemyss my mother;
And a' the folk about the house
To me were sister and brother.'
30.
30.[4] 'tyne,' lose.
'If the Earl of Wemyss was your father,
I wot sae he was mine;
And it shall not be for lack o' gowd

That ye your love sall tyne.

31.

'For I have seven ships o' mine ain,

A' loaded to the brim,

And I will gie them a' to thee,

Wi' four to thine eldest son:

But thanks to a' the powers in heaven

That I gae maiden hame!'

THE CRUEL MOTHER

THE TEXT is given from Motherwell's *Minstrelsy*, earlier versions being only fragmentary.

THE STORY has a close parallel in a Danish ballad; and another, popular all over Germany, is a variation of the same theme, but in place of the mother's final doom being merely mentioned, in the German ballad she is actually carried away by the devil.

In a small group of ballads, the penknife appears to be the ideal weapon for murder or suicide. See the *Twa Brothers* and the *Bonny Hind*.

THE CRUEL MOTHER

1.

SHE leaned her back unto a thorn;

Three, three, and three by three

And there she has her two babes born.

Three, three, and thirty-three.

2.

She took frae 'bout her ribbon-belt,

And there she bound them hand and foot.

3.

She has ta'en out her wee pen-knife,

And there she ended baith their life.

4.

She has howked a hole baith deep and wide,

She has put them in baith side by side.

5.

She has covered them o'er wi' a marble stane,

Thinking she would gang maiden hame.

6.

As she was walking by her father's castle wa',

She saw twa pretty babes playing at the ba'.

7.

'O bonnie babes, gin ye were mine,

I would dress you up in satin fine.

8.

'O I would dress you in the silk,

And wash you ay in morning milk.'

9.

9.[2] 'twine,' coarse cloth; *i.e.* shroud.

'O cruel mother, we were thine,

And thou made us to wear the twine.

10.

'O cursed mother, heaven's high,

And that's where thou will ne'er win nigh.

11.

'O cursed mother, hell is deep,

And there thou'll enter step by step.'

CHILD WATERS

THE TEXT is here given from the Percy Folio, with some emendations as suggested by Child.

THE STORY, if we omit the hard tests imposed on the maid's affection, is widely popular in a series of Scandinavian ballads,—Danish, Swedish, and Norwegian; and Percy's edition (in the *Reliques*) was popularised in Germany by Bürger's translation.

The disagreeable nature of the final insult (stt. 27-29), retained here only for the sake of fidelity to the original text, may be paralleled by the similarly sudden lapse of taste in the *Nut-Brown Maid*. We can but hope—as indeed is probable—that the objectionable lines are in each case interpolated.

'Child,' as in 'Child Roland,' etc., is a title of courtesy = Knight.

CHILD WATERS

1.

CHILDE WATTERS in his stable stoode,

& stroaket his milke-white steede;

To him came a ffaire young ladye

As ere did weare womans weede.

2.

2.² 'see,' protect. So constantly in this phrase.

Saies, 'Christ you saue, good Chyld Waters!'

Sayes, 'Christ you saue and see!

My girdle of gold which was too longe

Is now to short ffor mee.

3.

'& all is with one chyld of yours,

I ffeele sturre att my side:

My gowne of greene, it is to strayght;

Before it was to wide.'

4.

'If the child be mine, faire Ellen,' he sayd,

'Be mine, as you tell mee,

Take you Cheshire & Lancashire both,

Take them your owne to bee.

5.

'If the child be mine, ffaire Ellen,' he said,

'Be mine, as you doe sweare,

Take you Cheshire & Lancashire both,

& make that child your heyre.'

6.

Shee saies, 'I had rather haue one kisse,

Child Waters, of thy mouth,

Then I would have Cheshire & Lancashire both,

That lyes by north & south.

7.

'& I had rather haue a twinkling,

Child Waters, of your eye,

Then I would have Cheshire & Lancashire both,

To take them mine oune to bee!'

8.

'To-morrow, Ellen, I must forth ryde

Soe ffar into the north countrye;

The ffairest lady that I can ffind,

Ellen, must goe with mee.'

'& euer I pray you, Child Watters,

Your ffootpage let me bee!'

9.

'If you will my ffootpage be, Ellen,

As you doe tell itt mee,

Then you must cut your gownne of greene
An inch aboue your knee.

10.

'Soe must you doe your yellow lockes
Another inch aboue your eye;
You must tell no man what is my name;
My ffootpage then you shall bee.'

11.

All this long day Child Waters rode,
Shee ran bare ffoote by his side;
Yett was he neuer soe curteous a knight,
To say, 'Ellen, will you ryde?'

12.

But all this day Child Waters rode,
She ran barffoote thorow the broome!
Yett he was neuer soe curteous a knight
As to say, 'Put on your shoone.'

13.

'Ride softlye,' shee said, 'Child Watters:
Why do you ryde soe ffast?
The child, which is no mans but yours,
My bodye itt will burst.'

14.

He sayes, 'Sees thou yonder water, Ellen,
That fflowes from banke to brim?'
'I trust to God, Child Waters,' shee sayd,
'You will neuer see mee swime.'

15.

But when shee came to the waters side,

Shee sayled to the chinne:

'Except the lord of heauen be my speed,

Now must I learne to swime.'

16.

The salt waters bare vp Ellens clothes,

Our Ladye bare vpp her chinne,

& Child Waters was a woe man, good Lord,

To ssee faire Ellen swime.

17.

& when shee ouer the water was,

Shee then came to his knee:

He said, 'Come hither, ffaire Ellen,

Loe yonder what I see!

18.

18.² 'yates,' gates.

18.³ In each case the Folio gives '24' for 'four and twenty.'

18.⁴ 'wordlye make,' worldly mate.

'Seest thou not yonder hall, Ellen?

Of redd gold shine the yates;

There's four and twenty ffayre ladyes,

The ffairest is my wordlye make.

19.

'Seest thou not yonder hall, Ellen?

Of redd gold shineth the tower;

There is four and twenty ffaire ladyes,

The fairest is my paramoure.'

20.

'I doe see the hall now, Child Waters,

That of redd gold shineth the yates;

God giue good then of your selfe,

& of your wordlye make!

21.

'I doe see the hall now, Child Waters,

That of redd gold shineth the tower;

God giue good then of your selfe,

And of your paramoure!'

22.

There were four and twenty ladyes,

Were playing att the ball;

& Ellen, was the ffairest ladye,

Must bring his steed to the stall.

23.

There were four and twenty faire ladyes

Was playing att the chesse;

& Ellen, shee was the ffairest ladye,

Must bring his horsse to grasse.

24.

& then bespake Child Waters sister,

& these were the words said shee:

'You haue the prettyest ffootpage, brother,

That ever I saw with mine eye;

25.

'But that his belly it is soe bigg,

His girdle goes wonderous hye;

& euer I pray you, Child Waters,

Let him go into the chamber with me.'

26.

26.⁶ 'rich' added by Percy.

28.⁶ 'For filinge,' to save defiling.

'It is more meete for a litle ffootpage,

That has run through mosse and mire,

To take his supper vpon his knee

& sitt downe by the kitchin fyer,

Then to go into the chamber with any ladye

That weares so [rich] attyre.'

27.

But when thé had supped euery one,

To bedd they tooke the way;

He sayd, 'Come hither, my litle footpage,

Hearken what I doe say!

28.

'& goe thee downe into yonder towne,

& low into the street;

The ffarest ladye that thou can find,

Hyer her in mine armes to sleepe,

& take her vp in thine armes two,

For filinge of her ffeete.'

29.

Ellen is gone into the towne,

& low into the streete:

The fairest ladye that shee cold find

She hyred in his armes to sleepe,

& tooke her in her armes two,

For filing of her ffeete.

30.

30.⁴ 'say,' essay, attempt.

'I pray you now, good Child Waters,

That I may creepe in att your bedds feete,

For there is noe place about this house

Where I may say a sleepe.'

31.

31.[1] 'night.' Child's emendation. Percy read: 'This done, the nighte drove on apace.'

This [night] & itt droue on afftterward

Till itt was neere the day:

He sayd, 'Rise vp, my litle ffoote page,

& giue my steed corne & hay;

& soe doe thou the good blacke oates,

That he may carry me the better away.'

32.

32.[3] 'and'; Folio *on*.

And vp then rose ffaire Ellen,

& gave his steed corne & hay,

& soe shee did and the good blacke oates,

That he might carry him the better away.

33.

Shee layned her backe to the manger side,

& greiuouslye did groane;

& that beheard his mother deere,

And heard her make her moane.

34.

Shee said, 'Rise vp, thou Child Waters!

I thinke thou art a cursed man;

For yonder is a ghost in thy stable,

That greiuously doth groane,

Or else some woman laboures of child,

Shee is soe woe begone!'

35.

But vp then rose Child Waters,

& did on his shirt of silke;

Then he put on his other clothes

On his body as white as milke.

36.

36.[4] 'monand,' moaning.

& when he came to the stable dore,

Full still that hee did stand,

That hee might heare now faire Ellen,

How shee made her monand.

37.

Shee said, 'Lullabye, my owne deere child!

Lullabye, deere child, deere!

I wold thy father were a king,

Thy mother layd on a beere!'

38.

'Peace now,' he said, 'good faire Ellen!

& be of good cheere, I thee pray,

& the bridall & the churching both,

They shall bee vpon one day.'

EARL BRAND, THE DOUGLAS TRAGEDY, and THE CHILD OF ELL

THERE are here put in juxtaposition three versions in ballad-form of the same story, though fragmentary in the two latter cases, not only because each is good, but to show the possibilities of variation in a popular story. There is yet another ballad, *Erlinton*, printed by Sir Walter Scott in the *Minstrelsy*, embodying an almost identical tale. *Earl Brand* preserves most of the features of a very ancient story with more exactitude than any other traditional ballad. But in this case, as in too many others, we must turn to a Scandinavian ballad for the complete form of the story. A Danish ballad, *Ribold and Guldborg*, gives the fine tale thus:—

Ribold, a king's son, in love with Guldborg, offers to carry her away 'to a land where death and sorrow come not, where all the birds are cuckoos, where all the grass is leeks, where all the streams run with wine.' Guldborg is willing, but doubts whether she can escape the strict watch kept over her by her family and by her betrothed lover. Ribold disguises her in his armour and a cloak, and they ride away. On the moor they meet an earl, who asks, 'Whither away?' Ribold answers that he is taking his youngest sister from a cloister. This does not deceive the earl, nor does a bribe close his mouth; and Guldborg's father, learning that she is away with Ribold, rides with his sons in pursuit. Ribold bids Guldborg hold his horse, and prepares to fight; he tells her that, whatever may chance, she must not call on him by name. Ribold slays her father and some of her kin and six of her brothers; only her youngest brother is left: Guldborg cries, 'Ribold, spare him,' that he may carry tidings to her mother. Immediately Ribold receives a mortal wound. He ceases fighting, sheathes his sword, and says to her, 'Wilt thou go home to thy mother again, or wilt thou follow so sad a swain?' And she says she will follow him. In silence they ride on. 'Why art not thou merry as before?' asks Guldborg. And Ribold answers, 'Thy brother's sword has been in my heart.' They reach his house: he calls for one to take his horse, another to fetch a priest; for his brother shall have Guldborg. But she refuses. That night dies Ribold, and Guldborg slays herself and dies in his arms.

A second and even more dramatic ballad, *Hildebrand and Hilde*, tells a similar story.

A comparison of the above tale with *Earl Brand* will show a close agreement in most of the incidents. The chief loss in the English ballad is the request of Ribold, that Guldborg must not speak his name while he fights. The very name 'Brand' is doubtless a direct derivative of 'Hildebrand.' Winchester (13.²), as it implies a nunnery, corresponds to the cloister in the Danish ballad. Earl Brand directs his mother to marry the King's daughter to his youngest brother; but her refusal, if she did as Guldborg did, has been lost.

The Douglas Tragedy, a beautiful but fragmentary version, is, says Scott, 'one of the few to which popular tradition has ascribed complete locality.' The ascribed locality, if more complete, is no more probable than any other: to ascribe any definite locality to a ballad is in all cases a waste of time and labour.

The Child of Ell, in the Percy Folio, *may* have contained anything; but immediately we approach a point where comparison would be of interest, we meet an *hiatus valde deflendus*. Percy, in the *Reliques*, expanded the fragment here given to about five times the length.

EARL BRAND

(From R. BELL'S *Ancient Poems, Ballads*, etc.)

1.

OH did ye ever hear o' brave Earl Bran'?

Ay lally, o lilly lally

He courted the king's daughter of fair England

All i' the night sae early.

2.

She was scarcely fifteen years of age

Till sae boldly she came to his bedside.

3.

'O Earl Bran', fain wad I see

A pack of hounds let loose on the lea.'

4.

'O lady, I have no steeds but one,

And thou shalt ride, and I will run.'

5.

'O Earl Bran', my father has two,

And thou shall have the best o' them a'.'

6.

They have ridden o'er moss and moor,

And they met neither rich nor poor.

7.

Until they met with old Carl Hood;

He comes for ill, but never for good.

8.

'Earl Bran', if ye love me,

Seize this old earl, and gar him die.'

9.

'O lady fair, it wad be sair,

To slay an old man that has grey hair.

10.

'O lady fair, I'll no do sae,

I'll gie him a pound and let him gae.'

11.

'O where hae ye ridden this lee lang day?

O where hae ye stolen this lady away?'

12.

'I have not ridden this lee lang day,

Nor yet have I stolen this lady away.

13.

'She is my only, my sick sister,

Whom I have brought from Winchester.'

14.

'If she be sick, and like to dead,

Why wears she the ribbon sae red?

15.

'If she be sick, and like to die,

Then why wears she the gold on high?'

16.

When he came to this lady's gate,

Sae rudely as he rapped at it.

17.

'O where's the lady o' this ha'?'

'She's out with her maids to play at the ba'.'

18.

'Ha, ha, ha! ye are a' mista'en:

Gae count your maidens o'er again.

19.

'I saw her far beyond the moor

Away to be the Earl o' Bran's whore.'

20.

The father armed fifteen of his best men,

To bring his daughter back again.

21.

O'er her left shoulder the lady looked then:

'O Earl Bran', we both are tane.'

22.

'If they come on me ane by ane,

Ye may stand by and see them slain.

23.

'But if they come on me one and all,

Ye may stand by and see me fall.'

24.

They have come on him ane by ane,

And he has killed them all but ane.

25.

And that ane came behind his back,

And he's gi'en him a deadly whack.

26.

But for a' sae wounded as Earl Bran' was,

He has set his lady on her horse.

27.

They rode till they came to the water o' Doune,

And then he alighted to wash his wounds.

28.

'O Earl Bran', I see your heart's blood!'

''Tis but the gleat o' my scarlet hood.'

29.

They rode till they came to his mother's gate,

And sae rudely as he rapped at it.

30.

'O my son's slain, my son's put down,

And a' for the sake of an English loun.'

31.

'O say not sae, my dear mother,

But marry her to my youngest brother.

32.

'This has not been the death o' ane,

But it's been that o' fair seventeen.'

THE DOUGLAS TRAGEDY

(From SCOTT'S *Minstrelsy*)

1.

'RISE up, rise up now, Lord Douglas,' she says,

'And put on your armour so bright;

Let it never be said that a daughter of thine

Was married to a lord under night.

2.

'Rise up, rise up, my seven bold sons,

And put on your armour so bright;

And take better care of your youngest sister,

For your eldest's awa' the last night!'

3.

He's mounted her on a milk-white steed,

And himself on a dapple grey,

With a bugelet horn hung down by his side,

And lightly they rode away.

4.

Lord William lookit o'er his left shoulder,

To see what he could see,

And there he spy'd her seven brethren bold

Come riding over the lee.

5.

'Light down, light down, Lady Margret,' he said,

'And hold my steed in your hand,

Until that against your seven brethren bold,

And your father, I mak' a stand.'

6.

She held his steed in her milk-white hand,

And never shed one tear,

Until that she saw her seven brethren fa',

And her father hard fighting, who lov'd her so dear.

7.

'O hold your hand, Lord William!' she said,

'For your strokes they are wondrous sair;

True lovers I can get many a ane,

But a father I can never get mair.'

8.

8.3 'dighted,' dressed.

O she's ta'en out her handkerchief,

It was o' the holland sae fine,

And aye she dighted her father's bloody wounds,

That were redder than the wine.

9.

'O chuse, O chuse, Lady Margret,' he said,

'O whether will ye gang or bide?'

'I'll gang, I'll gang, Lord William,' she said,

'For ye have left me no other guide.'

10.

He's lifted her on a milk-white steed,

And himself on a dapple grey,

With a bugelet horn hung down by his side,

And slowly they baith rade away.

11.

O they rade on, and on they rade,

And a' by the light of the moon,

Until they came to yon wan water,

And there they lighted down.

12.

They lighted down to tak' a drink

Of the spring that ran sae clear:

And down the stream ran his gude heart's blood,

And sair she gan to fear.

13.

'Hold up, hold up, Lord William,' she says,

'For I fear that you are slain!'

''Tis naething but the shadow of my scarlet cloak,

That shines in the water sae plain.'

14.

O they rade on, and on they rade,

And a' by the light of the moon,

Until they cam' to his mother's ha' door,

And there they lighted down.

15.

'Get up, get up, lady mother,' he says,

'Get up, and let me in!

Get up, get up, lady mother,' he says,

'For this night my fair ladye I've win.

16.

'O mak' my bed, lady mother,' he says,

'O mak' it braid and deep,

And lay Lady Margret close at my back,

And the sounder I will sleep.'

17.

Lord William was dead lang ere midnight,

Lady Margret lang ere day,

And all true lovers that go thegither,

May they have mair luck than they!

18.

Lord William was buried in St. Mary's kirk,

Lady Margret in Mary's quire;

Out o' the lady's grave grew a bonny red rose,

And out o' the knight's a briar.

19.

And they twa met, and they twa plat,
And fain they wad be near;
And a' the warld might ken right weel,
They were twa lovers dear.

20.

But bye and rade the Black Douglas,
And wow but he was rough!
For he pull'd up the bonny brier,
And flang't in St. Mary's Loch.

THE CHILD OF ELL

(Fragment: from the Percy Folio)

1.[3] The maiden is speaking.

1.

. . . . .

. . . . .

Sayes, 'Christ thee saue, good child of Ell,
Christ saue thee & thy steede!

2.

'My father sayes he will noe meate,
Nor his drinke shall doe him noe good,
Till he haue slaine the child of Ell,
& haue seene his hart's blood.'

3.

'I wold I were in my sadle sett,
& a mile out of the towne,
I did not care for your father
& all his merrymen.

4.

'I wold I were in my sadle sett

& a litle space him froe,

I did not care for your father

& all that long him to!'

5.

5.⁴ 'blend,' blended, mixed.

He leaned ore his saddle bow,

To kisse this lady good;

The teares that went them 2 betweene

Were blend water & blood.

6.

6.² 'on': the MS. gives 'of.'

He sett himselfe on one good steed,

This lady on one palfray,

& sett his litle horne to his mouth,

& roundlie he rode away.

7.

He had not ridden past a mile,

A mile out of the towne,

Her father was readye with her 7 brether,

He said, 'Sett thou my daughter downe!

For it ill beseemes thee, thou false churles sonne,

To carry her forth of this towne!'

8.

'But lowd thou lyest, Sir Iohn the Knight,

Thou now doest lye of me;

A knight me gott, & a lady me bore;

Soe neuer did none by thee.

9.

'But light now downe, my lady gay,

Light downe & hold my horsse,

Whilest I & your father & your brether

Doe play vs at this crosse.

10.

10.³ The rest (about nine stt.) is missing.

'But light now downe, my owne trew loue,

& meeklye hold my steede,

Whilest your father [and your brether] bold

.   .   .   .   .

LORD THOMAS AND FAIR ANNET

THE TEXT is from Percy's *Reliques* (vol. ii., 1765: vol. iii., 1767). In the latter edition he also gives the English version of the ballad earlier in the same volume.

THE STORY.—This ballad, as it is one of the most beautiful, is also one of the most popular. It should be compared with *Fair Margaret and Sweet William*, in which the forlorn maid dies of grief, not by the hand of her rival.

A series of Norse ballads tell much the same tale, but in none is the 'friends' will' a crucial point. Chansons from Burgundy, Bretagne, Provence, and northern Italy, faintly echo the story.

Lord Thomas his mither says that Fair Annet has no 'gowd and gear'; yet later on we find that Annet's father can provide her with a horse shod with silver and gold, and four-and-twenty silver bells in his mane; she is attended by a large company, her cleading skinkles, and her belt is of pearl.

LORD THOMAS AND FAIR ANNET

1.

LORD THOMAS and Fair Annet

Sate a' day on a hill;

Whan night was cum, and sun was sett,

They had not talkt their fill.

2.

Lord Thomas said a word in jest,

Fair Annet took it ill:

'A, I will nevir wed a wife

Against my ain friends' will.'

3.

'Gif ye wull nevir wed a wife,

A wife wull neir wed yee':

Sae he is hame to tell his mither,

And knelt upon his knee.

4.

4.[1] 'rede,' advise.

4.[3] 'nut-browne' here = dusky, not fair; cp.:—
'In the old age black was not counted fair.'
—SHAKESPEARE, *Sonnet* CXXVII.

'O rede, O rede, mither,' he says,

'A gude rede gie to mee:

O sall I tak the nut-browne bride,

And let Faire Annet bee?'

5.

'The nut-browne bride haes gowd and gear,

Fair Annet she has gat nane;

And the little beauty Fair Annet haes,

O it wull soon be gane.'

6.

And he has till his brother gane:

'Now, brother, rede ye mee;

A, sall I marrie the nut-browne bride,

And let Fair Annet bee?'

7.

'The nut-browne bride has oxen, brother,

The nut-browne bride has kye:

I wad hae ye marrie the nut-browne bride,

And cast Fair Annet bye.'

8.

8.[4] 'fadge,' *lit.* a thick cake; here figuratively for the thick-set 'nut-browne bride.'

'Her oxen may dye i' the house, billie,

And her kye into the byre,

And I sall hae nothing to mysell

Bot a fat fadge by the fyre.'

9.

And he has till his sister gane:

'Now sister, rede ye mee;

O sall I marrie the nut-browne bride,

And set Fair Annet free?'

10.

'I'se rede ye tak Fair Annet, Thomas,

And let the browne bride alane;

Lest ye sould sigh, and say, Alace,

What is this we brought hame!'

11.

'No, I will tak my mither's counsel,

And marrie me owt o' hand;

And I will tak the nut-browne bride;

Fair Annet may leive the land.'

12.

Up then rose Fair Annet's father,

Twa hours or it wer day,

And he is gane into the bower

Wherein Fair Annet lay.

13.

'Rise up, rise up, Fair Annet,' he says,

'Put on your silken sheene;

Let us gae to St. Marie's kirke,

And see that rich weddeen.'

14.

'My maides, gae to my dressing-roome,

And dress to me my hair;

Whaireir yee laid a plait before,

See yee lay ten times mair.

15.

'My maides, gae to my dressing-room,

And dress to me my smock;

The one half is o' the holland fine,

The other o' needle-work.'

16.

The horse Fair Annet rade upon,

He amblit like the wind;

Wi' siller he was shod before,

Wi' burning gowd behind.

17.

17.³ 'yae tift,' [at] every puff.

Four and twenty siller bells

Wer a' tyed till his mane,

And yae tift o' the norland wind,

They tinkled ane by ane.

18.

Four and twenty gay gude knichts

Rade by Fair Annet's side,

And four and twenty fair ladies,

As gin she had bin a bride.

19.

19.² 'stean,' stone.

19.³ 'cleading,' clothing.

19.⁴ 'skinkled,' glittered.

And whan she cam to Marie's kirk,

She sat on Marie's stean:

The cleading that Fair Annet had on

It skinkled in their een.

20.

And whan she cam into the kirk,

She shimmered like the sun;

The belt that was about her waist,

Was a' wi' pearles bedone.

21.

She sat her by the nut-browne bride,

And her een they wer sae clear,

Lord Thomas he clean forgat the bride,

Whan Fair Annet drew near.

22.

He had a rose into his hand,

He gae it kisses three,

And reaching by the nut-browne bride,

Laid it on Fair Annet's knee.

23.

Up than spak the nut-browne bride,

She spak wi' meikle spite:

'And whair gat ye that rose-water,

That does mak yee sae white?'

24.

24.3,4 *i.e.* I was born fair.

'O I did get the rose-water

Whair ye wull neir get nane,

For I did get that very rose-water

Into my mither's wame.'

25.

The bride she drew a long bodkin

Frae out her gay head-gear,

And strake Fair Annet unto the heart,

That word spak nevir mair.

26.

26.[4] 'wood-wroth,' raging mad.

Lord Thomas he saw Fair Annet wex pale,

And marvelit what mote bee;

But whan he saw her dear heart's blude,

A' wood-wroth wexed hee.

27.

He drew his dagger, that was sae sharp,

That was sae sharp and meet,

And drave it into the nut-browne bride,

That fell deid at his feit.

28.

'Now stay for me, dear Annet,' he sed,

'Now stay, my dear,' he cry'd;

Then strake the dagger untill his heart,

And fell deid by her side.

29.

29, 30. This conclusion to a tragic tale of true-love is common to many ballads; see *Fair Margaret and Sweet William* and especially *Lord Lovel*.

Lord Thomas was buried without kirk-wa',

Fair Annet within the quiere,

And o' the tane thair grew a birk,

The other a bonny briere.

30.

30.[1] 'threw,' intertwined.

And ay they grew, and ay they threw,

As they wad faine be neare;

And by this ye may ken right weil

They were twa luvers deare.

THE BROWN GIRL

THE TEXT of this ballad was taken down before the end of the nineteenth century by the Rev. S. Baring Gould, from a blacksmith at Thrushleton, Devon.

THE STORY is a simple little tale which recalls *Barbara Allen*, *Clerk Sanders*, *Lord Thomas and Fair Annet*, and others. I have placed it here for contrast, and in illustration of the disdain of 'brown' maids.

THE BROWN GIRL

1.

'I AM as brown as brown can be,

And my eyes as black as sloe;

I am as brisk as brisk can be,

And wild as forest doe.

2.

'My love he was so high and proud,

His fortune too so high,

He for another fair pretty maid

Me left and passed me by.

3.

'Me did he send a love-letter,

He sent it from the town,

Saying no more he loved me,

For that I was so brown.

4.

'I sent his letter back again,

Saying his love I valued not,

Whether that he would fancy me,

Whether that he would not.

5.

'When that six months were overpass'd,
Were overpass'd and gone,
Then did my lover, once so bold,
Lie on his bed and groan.

6.

'When that six months were overpass'd,
Were gone and overpass'd,
O then my lover, once so bold,
With love was sick at last.

7.

'First sent he for the doctor-man:
"You, doctor, me must cure;
The pains that now do torture me
I can not long endure."

8.

'Next did he send from out the town,
O next did send for me;
He sent for me, the brown, brown girl
Who once his wife should be.

9.

'O ne'er a bit the doctor-man
His sufferings could relieve;
O never an one but the brown, brown girl
Who could his life reprieve.'

10.

Now you shall hear what love she had
For this poor love-sick man,
How all one day, a summer's day,
She walked and never ran.

11.

When that she came to his bedside,

Where he lay sick and weak,

O then for laughing she could not stand

Upright upon her feet.

12.

'You flouted me, you scouted me,

And many another one,

Now the reward is come at last,

For all that you have done.'

13.

The rings she took from off her hands,

The rings by two and three:

'O take, O take these golden rings,

By them remember me.'

14.

She had a white wand in her hand,

She strake him on the breast:

'My faith and troth I give back to thee,

So may thy soul have rest.'

15.

'Prithee,' said he, 'forget, forget,

Prithee forget, forgive;

O grant me yet a little space,

That I may be well and live.'

16.

'O never will I forget, forgive,
So long as I have breath;
I'll dance above your green, green grave
Where you do lie beneath.'

FAIR MARGARET AND SWEET WILLIAM

THE TEXT is from a broadside in the Douce Ballads, with a few unimportant corrections from other stall-copies, as printed by Percy and Ritson.

THE STORY is much the same as *Lord Thomas and Fair Annet*, except in the manner of Margaret's death.

None of the known copies of the ballad are as early in date as *The Knight of the Burning Pestle* (a play by Beaumont and Fletcher, first produced, it is said, in 1611), in which the humorous old Merrythought sings two fragments of this ballad; stanza 5 in Act II. Sc. 8, and the first two lines of stanza 2 in Act III. Sc. 5. As there given, the lines are slightly different.

The last four stanzas of this ballad again present the stock ending, for which see the introduction to *Lord Lovel*. The last stanza condemns itself.

FAIR MARGARET AND SWEET WILLIAM

1.

As it fell out on a long summer's day,

Two lovers they sat on a hill;

They sat together that long summer's day,

And could not talk their fill.

2.

'I see no harm by you, Margaret,

Nor you see none by me;

Before tomorrow eight a clock

A rich wedding shall you see.'

3.

Fair Margaret sat in her bower-window,

A combing of her hair,

And there she spy'd Sweet William and his bride,

As they were riding near.

4.

Down she lay'd her ivory comb,

And up she bound her hair;

She went her way forth of her bower,

But never more did come there.

5.

When day was gone, and night was come,

And all men fast asleep,

Then came the spirit of Fair Margaret,

And stood at William's feet.

6.

'God give you joy, you two true lovers,

In bride-bed fast asleep;

Loe I am going to my green grass grave,

And am in my winding-sheet.'

7.

When day was come, and night was gone,

And all men wak'd from sleep,

Sweet William to his lady said,

'My dear, I have cause to weep.

8.

'I dream'd a dream, my dear lady;

Such dreams are never good;

I dream'd my bower was full of red swine,

And my bride-bed full of blood.'

9.

'Such dreams, such dreams, my honoured lord,

They never do prove good,

To dream thy bower was full of swine,

And thy bride-bed full of blood.'

10.

He called up his merry men all,

By one, by two, and by three,

Saying, 'I'll away to Fair Margaret's bower,

By the leave of my lady.'

11.

And when he came to Fair Margaret's bower,

He knocked at the ring;

So ready was her seven brethren

To let Sweet William in.

12.

He turned up the covering-sheet:

'Pray let me see the dead;

Methinks she does look pale and wan,

She has lost her cherry red.

13.

'I'll do more for thee, Margaret,

Than any of thy kin;

For I will kiss thy pale wan lips,

Tho' a smile I cannot win.'

14.

With that bespeak her seven brethren,

Making most pitious moan:

'You may go kiss your jolly brown bride,

And let our sister alone.'

15.

'If I do kiss my jolly brown bride,

I do but what is right;

For I made no vow to your sister dear,

By day or yet by night.

16.

'Pray tell me then how much you'll deal

Of your white bread and your wine;

So much as is dealt at her funeral today

Tomorrow shall be dealt at mine.'

17.

Fair Margaret dy'd today, today,

Sweet William he dy'd the morrow;

Fair Margaret dy'd for pure true love,

Sweet William he dy'd for sorrow.

18.

Margaret was buried in the lower chancel,

Sweet William in the higher;

Out of her breast there sprung a rose,

And out of his a brier.

19.

They grew as high as the church-top,

Till they could grow no higher,

And then they grew in a true lover's knot,

Which made all people admire.

20.

There came the clerk of the parish,

As you this truth shall hear,

And by misfortune cut them down,

Or they had now been there.

LORD LOVEL

'It is silly sooth,

And dallies with the innocence of love,

Like the old age.'

—*Twelfth Night*, II. 4.

THE TEXT.—This ballad, concluding a small class of three—*Lord Thomas and Fair Annet*, and *Fair Margaret and Sweet William* being the other two—is distinguished by the fact that the lady dies of hope deferred. It is a foolish ballad, at the opposite pole to *Lord Thomas and Fair Annet*, and is pre-eminently one of the class meant only to be sung, with an effective burden. The text given here, therefore, is that of a broadside of the year 1846.

THE STORY in outline is extremely popular in German and Scandinavian literature. Of the former the commonest is *Der Ritter und die Maid*, also found north of Germany; twenty-six different versions in all, in some of which lilies spring from the grave. In a Swedish ballad a linden-tree grows out of their bodies; in Danish ballads, roses, lilies, or lindens. This conclusion, a commonplace in folk-song, occurs also in a class of Romaic ballads, where a clump of reeds rises from one of the lovers, and a cypress or lemon-tree from the other, which bend to each other and mingle their leaves whenever the wind blows. Classical readers will recall the tale of Philemon and Baucis.

For further information on this subject, consult the special section of the Introduction.

Various other versions of this ballad are named *Lady Ouncebell*, *Lord Lavel*, *Lord Travell*, and *Lord Revel*.

LORD LOVEL

1.

1.4,5 A similar repetition of the last line of each verse makes the refrain throughout.

LORD LOVEL he stood at his castle-gate,

Combing his milk-white steed,

When up came Lady Nancy Belle,

To wish her lover good speed, speed,

To wish her lover good speed.

2.

'Where are you going, Lord Lovel?' she said,

'Oh where are you going?' said she;

'I'm going, my Lady Nancy Belle,

Strange countries for to see.'

3.

'When will you be back, Lord Lovel?' she said,

'Oh when will you come back?' said she;

'In a year, or two, or three at the most,

I'll return to my fair Nancy.'

4.

But he had not been gone a year and a day,

Strange countries for to see,

When languishing thoughts came into his head,

Lady Nancy Belle he would go see.

5.

So he rode, and he rode, on his milk-white steed,

Till he came to London town,

And there he heard St. Pancras' bells,

And the people all mourning round.

6.

'Oh what is the matter?' Lord Lovel he said,

'Oh what is the matter?' said he;

'A lord's lady is dead,' a woman replied,

'And some call her Lady Nancy.'

7.

So he ordered the grave to be opened wide,

And the shroud he turned down,

And there he kissed her clay-cold lips,

Till the tears came trickling down.

8.

Lady Nancy she died, as it might be, today,

Lord Lovel he died as tomorrow;

Lady Nancy she died out of pure, pure grief,

Lord Lovel he died out of sorrow.

9.

Lady Nancy was laid in St. Pancras' Church,

Lord Lovel was laid in the choir;

And out of her bosom there grew a red rose,

And out of her lover's a briar.

10.

10.[1] Perhaps a misprint for 'church-steeple top.'—CHILD.

They grew, and they grew, to the church-steeple too,

And then they could grow no higher;

So there they entwined in a true-lovers' knot,

For all lovers true to admire.

LADY MAISRY

THE TEXT.—From the Jamieson-Brown MS. All the other variants agree as to the main outline of the ballad.

THE STORY.—Lady Maisry, refusing the young lords of the north country, and saying that her love is given to an English lord, is suspected by her father's kitchy-boy, who goes to tell her brother. He charges her with her fault, reviles her for 'drawing up with an English lord,' and commands her to renounce him. She refuses, and is condemned to be burned. A bonny boy bears news of her plight to Lord William, who leaps to boot and saddle; but he arrives too late to save her, though he vows vengeance on all her kin, and promises to burn himself last of all.

Burning was the penalty usually allotted in the romances to a girl convicted of unchastity.

LADY MAISRY

1.

THE young lords o' the north country

Have all a wooing gone,

To win the love of Lady Maisry,

But o' them she woud hae none.

2.

O they hae courted Lady Maisry

Wi' a' kin kind of things;

An' they hae sought her Lady Maisry

Wi' brotches an' wi' rings.

3.

An' they ha' sought her Lady Maisry

Frae father and frae mother;

An' they ha' sought her Lady Maisry

Frae sister an' frae brother.

4.

An' they ha' follow'd her Lady Maisry
Thro' chamber an' thro' ha';
But a' that they coud say to her,
Her answer still was Na.

5.

5.¹ 'ha'd' = *haud*, hold.

'O ha'd your tongues, young men,' she says,
'An' think nae mair o' me;
For I've gi'en my love to an English lord,
An' think nae mair o' me.'

6.

Her father's kitchy-boy heard that,
An ill death may he dee!
An' he is on to her brother,
As fast as gang coud he.

7.

'O is my father an' my mother well,
But an' my brothers three?
Gin my sister Lady Maisry be well,
There's naething can ail me.'

8.

'Your father an' your mother is well,
But an' your brothers three;
Your sister Lady Maisry's well,
So big wi' bairn gangs she.'

9.

9.² 'mailison,' curse.

'Gin this be true you tell to me,
My mailison light on thee!

But gin it be a lie you tell,

You sal be hangit hie.'

10.

He's done him to his sister's bow'r,

Wi' meikle doole an' care;

An' there he saw her Lady Maisry

Kembing her yallow hair.

11.

11.[1] 'is aught,' owns.

'O wha is aught that bairn,' he says,

'That ye sae big are wi'?

And gin ye winna own the truth,

This moment ye sall dee.'

12.

She turn'd her right and roun' about,

An' the kem fell frae her han';

A trembling seiz'd her fair body,

An' her rosy cheek grew wan.

13.

'O pardon me, my brother dear,

An' the truth I'll tell to thee;

My bairn it is to Lord William,

An' he is betroth'd to me.'

14.

'O coud na ye gotten dukes, or lords,

Intill your ain country,

That ye draw up wi' an English dog,

To bring this shame on me?

15.

15.[4] 'forlorn,' forfeit.

'But ye maun gi' up the English lord,

Whan youre young babe is born;

For, gin you keep by him an hour langer,

Your life sall be forlorn.'

16.

'I will gi' up this English blood,

Till my young babe be born;

But the never a day nor hour langer,

Tho' my life should be forlorn.'

17.

'O whare is a' my merry young men,

Whom I gi' meat and fee,

To pu' the thistle and the thorn,

To burn this wile whore wi'?'

18.

'O whare will I get a bonny boy,

To help me in my need,

To rin wi' hast to Lord William,

And bid him come wi' speed?'

19.

O out it spake a bonny boy,

Stood by her brother's side:

'O I would run your errand, lady,

O'er a' the world wide.

20.

20.[2] *i.e.* in driving wind and rain.

'Aft have I run your errands, lady,

Whan blawn baith win' and weet;

But now I'll rin your errand, lady,

Wi' sa't tears on my cheek.'

21.

21. A stock ballad-stanza.

O whan he came to broken briggs,

He bent his bow and swam,

An' whan he came to the green grass growin',

He slack'd his shoone and ran.

22.

22.[2] 'baed,' stayed; 'chap,' knock.

22.[4] 'lap,' leapt.

O whan he came to Lord William's gates,

He baed na to chap or ca',

But set his bent bow till his breast,

An' lightly lap the wa';

An', or the porter was at the gate,

The boy was i' the ha'.

23.

23.[1] 'biggins,' buildings.

'O is my biggins broken, boy?

Or is my towers won?

Or is my lady lighter yet,

Of a dear daughter or son?'

24.

'Your biggin is na broken, sir,

Nor is your towers won;

But the fairest lady in a' the lan'

For you this day maun burn.'

25.

'O saddle me the black, the black,

Or saddle me the brown;

O saddle me the swiftest steed

That ever rade frae a town.'

26.

Or he was near a mile awa',

She heard his wild horse sneeze:

'Mend up the fire, my false brother,

It's na come to my knees.'

27.

O whan he lighted at the gate,

She heard his bridle ring;

'Mend up the fire, my false brother,

It's far yet frae my chin.

28.

'Mend up the fire to me, brother,

Mend up the fire to me;

For I see him comin' hard an' fast,

Will soon men' 't up to thee.

29.

29.[3] 'gleed,' burning coal, fire.

'O gin my hands had been loose, Willy,

Sae hard as they are boun',

I would have turn'd me frae the gleed,

And castin out your young son.'

30.

30.[1] 'gar,' make, cause.

'O I'll gar burn for you, Maisry,

Your father an' your mother;
An' I'll gar burn for you, Maisry,
Your sister an' your brother.

31.

'An' I'll gar burn for you, Maisry,
The chief of a' your kin;
An' the last bonfire that I come to,
Mysel' I will cast in.'

THE CRUEL BROTHER

THE TEXT is that obtained in 1800 by Alexander Fraser Tytler from Mrs. Brown of Falkland, and by him committed to writing. The first ten and the last two stanzas show corruption, but the rest of the ballad is in the best style.

THE STORY emphasises the necessity of asking the consent of a brother to the marriage of his sister, and therefore the title *The Cruel Brother* is a misnomer. In ballad-times, the brother would have been well within his rights; it was rather a fatal oversight of the bridegroom that caused the tragedy.

Danish and German ballads echo the story, though in the commonest German ballad, *Graf Friedrich*, the bride receives an *accidental* wound, and that from the bridegroom's own hand.

The testament of the bride, by which she benefits her friends and leaves curses on her enemies, is very characteristic of the ballad-style, and is found in other ballads, as *Lord Ronald* and *Edward, Edward*. In the present case, 'sister Grace' obtains what would seem to be a very doubtful benefit.

THE CRUEL BROTHER

1.

1.[2,4] It should be remembered that the refrain is supposed to be sung with each verse, here and elsewhere.

THERE was three ladies play'd at the ba',

With a hey ho and a lillie gay

There came a knight and played o'er them a',

As the primrose spreads so sweetly.

2.

The eldest was baith tall and fair,

But the youngest was beyond compare.

3.

The midmost had a graceful mien,

But the youngest look'd like beautie's queen.

4.

The knight bow'd low to a' the three,

But to the youngest he bent his knee.

5.

The ladie turned her head aside;

The knight he woo'd her to be his bride.

6.

The ladie blush'd a rosy red,

And say'd, 'Sir knight, I'm too young to wed.'

7.

'O ladie fair, give me your hand,

And I'll make you ladie of a' my land.'

8.

'Sir knight, ere ye my favour win,

You maun get consent frae a' my kin.'

9.

He's got consent frae her parents dear,

And likewise frae her sisters fair.

10.

He's got consent frae her kin each one,

But forgot to spiek to her brother John.

11.

Now, when the wedding day was come,

The knight would take his bonny bride home.

12.

And many a lord and many a knight

Came to behold that ladie bright.

13.

And there was nae man that did her see,

But wish'd himself bridegroom to be.

14.

Her father dear led her down the stair,

And her sisters twain they kiss'd her there.

15.

15.[1] 'closs,' close.

Her mother dear led her thro' the closs,

And her brother John set her on her horse.

16.

She lean'd her o'er the saddle-bow,

To give him a kiss ere she did go.

17.

He has ta'en a knife, baith lang and sharp,

And stabb'd that bonny bride to the heart.

18.

She hadno ridden half thro' the town,

Until her heart's blude stain'd her gown.

19.

'Ride softly on,' says the best young man,

'For I think our bonny bride looks pale and wan.'

20.

'O lead me gently up yon hill,

And I'll there sit down, and make my will.'

21.

'O what will you leave to your father dear?'

'The silver-shod steed that brought me here.'

22.

'What will you leave to your mother dear?'

'My velvet pall and my silken gear.'

23.

'What will you leave to your sister Anne?'

'My silken scarf and my gowden fan.'

24.

'What will you leave to your sister Grace?'

'My bloody cloaths to wash and dress.'

25.

'What will you leave to your brother John?'

'The gallows-tree to hang him on.'

26.

'What will you leave to your brother John's wife?'

'The wilderness to end her life.'

27.

This ladie fair in her grave was laid,

And many a mass was o'er her said.

28.

28.[2] 'rive,' tear.

But it would have made your heart right sair,

To see the bridegroom rive his hair.

THE NUTBROWN MAID

THE TEXT is from Arnold's *Chronicle*, of the edition which, from typographical evidence, is said to have been printed at Antwerp in 1502 by John Doesborowe. Each stanza is there printed in six long lines. Considerable variations appear in later editions. There is also a Balliol MS. (354), which contains a contemporary version, and the Percy Folio contains a corrupt version.

This should not be considered as a ballad proper; it is rather a 'dramatic lyric.' Its history, however, is quite as curious as that of many ballads. It occurs, as stated above, in the farrago known as the *Chronicle* of Richard Arnold, inserted between a list of the 'tolls' due on merchandise entering or leaving the port of Antwerp, and a table giving Flemish weights and moneys in terms of the corresponding English measures. Why such a poem should be printed in such incongruous surroundings, what its date or who its author was, are questions impossible to determine. Its position here is perhaps almost as incongruous as in its original place.

From 3.[9] to the end of the last verse but one, it is a dialogue between an earl's son and a baron's daughter, in alternate stanzas; a prologue and an epilogue are added by the author.

Matthew Prior printed the poem in his works, in order to contrast it with his own version, *Henry and Emma*, which appealed to contemporary taste as more elegant than its rude original.

THE NUTBROWN MAID

    1.

    1.[1] 'among,' from time to time.

    1.[5] 'neuer a dele,' not at all.

    BE it right, or wrong, these men among

    On women do complaine;

    Affermyng this, how that it is

    A labour spent in vaine,

    To loue them wele; for neuer a dele,

    They loue a man agayne;

    For lete a man do what he can,

Ther fouour to attayne,

Yet, yf a newe to them pursue,

Ther furst trew louer than

Laboureth for nought; and from her though[t]

He is a bannisshed man.

2.

I say not nay, bat that all day

It is bothe writ and sayde

That womans fayth is as who saythe

All utterly decayed;

But neutheles, right good wytnes

In this case might be layde;

That they loue trewe, and contynew,

Recorde the Nutbrowne maide:

Which from her loue, whan, her to proue,

He cam to make his mone,

Wolde not departe, for in her herte,

She louyd but hym allone.

3.

3.[4] 'they' = the. 'in fere,' in company. 'and fere' (= fear) is usually printed.

Than betwene us lete us discusse,

What was all the maner

Betwene them too; we wyll also

Tell all they payne in fere,

That she was in; now I begynne,

Soo that ye me answere;

Wherfore, ye, that present be

I pray you geue an eare.

I am the knyght; I cum be nyght,

As secret as I can;

Sayng, alas! thus stondyth the cause,

I am a bannisshed man.

4.

And I your wylle for to fulfylle

In this wyl not refuse;

Trusting to shewe, in wordis fewe,

That men haue an ille use

To ther owne shame wymen to blame,

And causeles them accuse;

Therfore to you I answere nowe,

All wymen to excuse,—

Myn owne hert dere, with you what chiere?

I prey you, tell anoon;

For, in my mynde, of all mankynde

I loue but you allon.

5.

5.¹ 'do,' done.

5.⁵ 'ton,' one.

5.¹⁰ *i.e.* I know no other advice.

It stondith so; a dede is do,

Wherfore moche harme shal growe;

My desteny is for to dey

A shamful dethe, I trowe;

Or ellis to flee: the ton must bee.

None other wey I knowe,

But to withdrawe as an outlaw,

And take me to my bowe.

Wherefore, adew, my owne hert trewe,

None other red I can:

For I muste to the grene wode goo,

Alone a bannysshed man.

6.

6.⁴ 'derked,' darkened.

6.⁷ 'wheder,' whither.

O Lorde, what is this worldis blisse,

That chaungeth as the mone!

My somers day in lusty may

Is derked before the none.

I here you saye farwel: nay, nay,

We depart not soo sone.

Why say ye so? wheder wyll ye goo?

Alas! what haue ye done?

Alle my welfare to sorow and care

Shulde chaunge, yf ye were gon;

For, in [my] mynde, of all mankynde

I loue but you alone.

7.

7.² 'distrayne,' affect.

7.⁵ 'aslake,' abate.

I can beleue, it shal you greue,

And somwhat you distrayne;

But, aftyrwarde, your paynes harde

Within a day or tweyne

Shall sone aslake; and ye shall take

Comfort to you agayne.

Why shuld ye nought? for, to make thought,

Your labur were in vayne.
And thus I do; and pray you, loo,
As hertely as I can;
For I must too the grene wode goo,
Alone a banysshed man.

8.
Now, syth that ye haue shewed to me
The secret of your mynde,
I shalbe playne to you agayne,
Lyke as ye shal me fynde.
Syth it is so, that ye wyll goo,
I wol not leue behynde;
Shall neuer be sayd, the Nutbrowne mayd,
Was to her loue unkind:
Make you redy, for soo am I,
All though it were anoon;
For, in my mynde, of all mankynde
I loue but you alone.

9.
Yet I you rede take good hede
Whan men wyl thynke, and sey;
Of yonge, and olde, it shalbe tolde,
That ye be gone away,
Your wanton wylle for to fulfylle,
In grene wood you to play;
And that ye myght from your delyte
Noo lenger make delay:
Rather than ye shuld thus for me
Be called an ylle woman,

Yet wolde I to the grene wodde goo,

Alone a banyshed man.

10.

10.9 'thoo,' those.

Though it be songe of olde and yonge,

That I shuld be to blame,

Theirs be the charge, that speke so large

In hurting of my name:

For I wyl proue that feythful loue

It is deuoyd of shame;

In your distresse and heuynesse,

To parte wyth you, the same:

And sure all thoo, that doo not so,

Trewe louers ar they noon;

But, in my mynde, of all mankynde

I loue but you alone.

11.

11.3 'renne,' run.

11.6 A later edition of the *Chronicle* reads— 'A bowe, redy to drawe.'

I councel yow, remembre howe

It is noo maydens lawe,

Nothing to dought, but to renne out

To wod with an outlawe;

For ye must there in your hande bere

A bowe to bere and drawe;

And, as a theef, thus must ye lyeue,

Euer in drede and awe,

By whiche to yow gret harme myght grow:

Yet had I leuer than,

That I had too the grenewod goo,

Alone a banysshyd man.

12.

I thinke not nay, but as ye saye,

It is noo maydens lore:

But loue may make me for your sake,

As ye haue said before

To com on fote, to hunte, and shote,

To gete us mete and store;

For soo that I your company

May haue, I aske noo more:

From whiche to parte, it makith myn herte

As colde as ony ston;

For, in my mynde, of all mankynde

I loue but you alone.

13.

13.[6] 'rescous,' rescue. Another edition has 'socurs.'

For an outlawe, this is the lawe,

That men hym take and binde;

Wythout pytee hanged to bee,

And wauer with the wynde.

Yf I had neede, (as God forbede!)

What rescous coude ye finde?

Forsothe, I trowe, you and your bowe

Shuld drawe for fere behynde:

And noo merueyle; for lytel auayle

Were in your councel than:

Wherfore I too the woode wyl goo

Alone a banysshd man.

- 121 -

14.

Ful wel knowe ye, that wymen bee

Ful febyl for to fyght;

Noo womanhed is it in deede

To bee bolde as a knight:

Yet, in suche fere, yf that ye were

Amonge enemys day and nyght,

I wolde wythstonde, with bowe in hande,

To greue them as I myght,

And you to saue; as wymen haue

From deth many one:

For, in my mynde, of all mankynde

I loue but you alone.

15.

15.[7] 'abowe,' above; 'roue,' roof.

Yet take good hede, for euer I drede

That ye coude not sustein

The thorney wayes, the depe valeis,

The snowe, the frost, the reyn,

The colde, the hete: for drye, or wete,

We must lodge on the playn;

And, us abowe, noon other roue

But a brake bussh or twayne:

Which sone shulde greue you, I beleue;

And ye wolde gladly than

That I had too the grenewode goo,

Alone a banysshyd man.

16.

Syth I haue here ben partynere

With you of joy and blysse,

I must also parte of your woo

Endure, as reason is:

Yet am I sure of oon plesure;

And, shortly, it is this:

That, where ye bee, me semeth, perde,

I coude not fare amysse,

Wythout more speche, I you beseche

That we were soon agone;

For, in my mynde, of all mankynde,

I loue but you alone.

17.

Yef ye goo thedyr, ye must consider,

Whan ye haue lust to dyne

Ther shal no mete before to gete,

Nor drinke, beer, ale, ne wine;

Ne shetis clene, to lye betwene,

Made of thred and twyne;

Noon other house but leuys and bowes

To keuer your hed and myn,

Loo, myn herte swete, this ylle dyet

Shuld make you pale and wan;

Wherfore I to the wood wyl goo,

Alone, a banysshid man.

18.

18.[7] 'hele,' health.

Amonge the wylde dere, suche an archier,

As men say that ye bee,

Ne may not fayle of good vitayle

Where is so grete plente:

And watir cleere of the ryuere

Shalbe ful swete to me;

Wyth whiche in hele I shal right wele

Endure, as ye shal see;

And, or we goo, a bed or twoo

I can prouide anoon;

For, in my mynde, of all mankynde

I loue but you alone.

19.

19.³ 'here,' hair; 'ere,' ear.

19.⁹ 'And,' If.

Loo, yet before ye must doo more,

Yf ye wyl goo with me;

As cutte your here up by your ere,

Your kirtel by the knee;

Wyth bowe in hande, for to withstonde

Your enmys, yf nede bee:

And this same nyght before daylyght,

To woodwarde wyl I flee.

And ye wyl all this fulfylle,

Doo it shortely as ye can:

Ellis wil I to the grenewode goo,

Alone, a banysshyd man.

20.

20.⁷ 'ensue,' follow.

I shal as now do more for you

That longeth to womanhed;

To short my here, a bowe to bere,

To shote in tyme of nede.

O my swete mod[er], before all other

For you haue I most drede:

But now, adiew! I must ensue

Wher fortune duth me leede.

All this make ye: now lete us flee;

The day cum fast upon;

For, in my mynde, of all mankynde

I loue but you alone.

21.

Nay, nay, not soo; ye shal not goo,

And I shal telle you why,—

Your appetyte is to be lyght

Of loue, I wele aspie:

For, right as ye haue sayd to me,

In lyke wyse hardely

Ye wolde answere who so euer it were,

In way of company.

It is sayd of olde, sone hote, sone colde;

And so is a woman.

Wherfore I too the woode wly goo,

Alone, a banysshid man.

22.

22.[2] The type is broken in the 1502 edition, which reads 'to say be....'

Yef ye take hede, yet is noo nede

Suche wordis to say by me;

For ofte ye preyd, and longe assayed,

Or I you louid, parde:

And though that I of auncestry

A barons doughter bee,

Yet haue you proued how I you loued

A squyer of lowe degree;

And euer shal, whatso befalle—

To dey therfore anoon;

For, in my mynde, of al mankynde

I loue but you alone.

23.

23.[6] 'yede,' went.

A barons childe to be begyled,

It were a curssed dede;

To be felow with an outlawe,

Almyghty God forbede.

Yet bettyr were the power squyere

Alone to forest yede,

Than ye shal saye another day,

That, be [my] wyked dede,

Ye were betrayed: wherfore, good maide,

The best red that I can,

Is, that I too the grenewode goo,

Alone, a banysshed man.

24.

Whatso euer befalle, I neuer shal

Of this thing you upbrayd:

But yf ye goo, and leue me soo,

Than haue ye me betraied.

Remembre you wele, how that ye dele

For, yf ye as the[y] sayd,

Be so unkynde, to leue behynde

Your loue, the notbrowne maide,

Trust me truly, that I [shall] dey

Sone after ye be gone;

For, in my mynde, of all mankynde

I loue but you alone.

25.

25.³ 'purueid (= purveyed) me,' provided myself.

Yef that ye went, ye shulde repent;

For in the forest nowe

I haue purueid me of a maide,

Whom I loue more than you;

Another fayrer, than euer ye were,

I dare it wel auowe;

And of you bothe eche shulde be wrothe

With other, as I trowe;

It were myn ease, to lyue in pease,

So wyl I, yf I can:

Wherfore I to the wode wyl goo,

Alone a banysshid man.

26.

26.⁹ 'moo' = mo, *i.e.* more.

Though in the wood I undirstode

Ye had a paramour,

All this may nought reineue my thought,

But that I wil be your;

And she shal fynde me soft and kynde,

And curteis euery our;

Glad to fulfylle all that she wylle

Commaunde me to my power:

For had ye, loo, an hundred moo,

Yet wolde I be that one,

For, in my mynde, of all mankynde,

I loue but you alone.

27.

Myn owne dere loue, I see the proue

That ye be kynde and trewe,

Of mayde, and wyf, in al my lyf,

The best that euer I knewe.

Be mery and glad, be no more sad,

The case is chaunged newe;

For it were ruthe, that, for your trouth,

Ye shuld haue cause to rewe.

Be not dismayed; whatsoeuer I sayd

To you, whan I began,

I wyl not too the grene wod goo,

I am noo banysshyd man.

28.

This tidingis be more glad to me,

Than to be made a quene,

Yf I were sure they shuld endure;

But it is often seen,

When men wyl breke promyse, they speke

The wordis on the splene;

Ye shape some wyle me to begyle

And stele fro me, I wene:

Than were the case wurs than it was,
And I more woobegone:
For, in my mynde, of al mankynde
I loue but you alone.

29.

Ye shal not nede further to drede;
I wyl not disparage
You, (God defende!) syth you descend
Of so grete a lynage.
Now understonde; to Westmerlande,
Whiche is my herytage,
I wyl you brynge; and wyth a rynge,
By wey of maryage
I wyl you take, and lady make,
As shortly as I can:
Thus haue ye wone an erles son
And not a banysshyd man.

30.

30.[10] 'echeon,' each one.

Here may ye see, that wymen be
In loue, meke, kinde, and stable;
Late neuer man repreue them than,
Or calle them variable;
But rather prey God that we may
To them be comfortable;

- 129 -

Whiche somtyme prouyth suche as loueth,
Yf they be charitable.
For sith men wolde that wymen sholde
Be meke to them echeon,
Moche more ought they to God obey,
And serue but Hym alone.

FAIR JANET

THE TEXT.—Of seven or eight variants of this ballad, only three preserve the full form of the story. On the whole, the one here given—from Sharp's *Ballad Book*, as sung by an old woman in Perthshire—is the best, as the other two—from Herd's *Scots Songs*, and the Kinloch MSS.—are slightly contaminated by extraneous matter.

THE STORY is a simple ballad-tale of 'true-love twinned'; but the episode of the dancing forms a link with a number of German and Scandinavian ballads, in which compulsory dancing and horse-riding is made a test of the guilt of an accused maiden. In the Scotch ballad the horse-riding has shrunk almost to nothing, and the dancing is not compulsory. The resemblance is faint, and the barbarities of the Continental versions are happily wanting in our ballad.

FAIR JANET

1.

'YE maun gang to your father, Janet,

Ye maun gang to him soon;

Ye maun gang to your father, Janet,

In case that his days are dune.'

2.

Janet's awa' to her father,

As fast as she could hie:

'O what's your will wi' me, father?

O what's your will wi' me?'

3.

'My will wi' you, Fair Janet,' he said,

'It is both bed and board;

Some say that ye lo'e Sweet Willie,

But ye maun wed a French lord.'

4.

'A French lord maun I wed, father?

A French lord maun I wed?

Then, by my sooth,' quo' Fair Janet,

'He's ne'er enter my bed.'

5.

5.4 'jo,' sweetheart.

Janet's awa' to her chamber,

As fast as she could go;

Wha's the first ane that tapped there,

But Sweet Willie her jo?

6.

'O we maun part this love, Willie,

That has been lang between;

There's a French lord coming o'er the sea,

To wed me wi' a ring;

There's a French lord coming o'er the sea,

To wed and tak' me hame.'

7.

'If we maun part this love, Janet,

It causeth mickle woe;

If we maun part this love, Janet,

It makes me into mourning go.'

8.

'But ye maun gang to your three sisters,

Meg, Marion, and Jean;

Tell them to come to Fair Janet,

In case that her days are dune.'

9.

Willie's awa' to his three sisters,

Meg, Marion, and Jean:

'O haste, and gang to Fair Janet,
I fear that her days are dune.'
10.
Some drew to them their silken hose,
Some drew to them their shoon,
Some drew to them their silk manteils,
Their coverings to put on,
And they're awa' to Fair Janet,
By the hie light o' the moon.

.   .   .   .   .

11.
'O I have born this babe, Willie,
Wi' mickle toil and pain;
Take hame, take hame, your babe, Willie,
For nurse I dare be nane.'
12.
He's tane his young son in his arms,
And kisst him cheek and chin,
And he's awa' to his mother's bower,
By the hie light o' the moon.
13.
'O open, open, mother,' he says,
'O open, and let me in;
The rain rains on my yellow hair,
And the dew drops o'er my chin,
And I hae my young son in my arms,
I fear that his days are dune.'

14.

With her fingers lang and sma'

She lifted up the pin,

And with her arms lang and sma'

Received the baby in.

15.

15.³ 'nourice,' nurse.

'Gae back, gae back now, Sweet Willie,

And comfort your fair lady;

For where ye had but ae nourice,

Your young son shall hae three.'

16.

16.⁴ 'busk,' dress.

Willie he was scarce awa',

And the lady put to bed,

When in and came her father dear:

'Make haste, and busk the bride.'

17.

'There's a sair pain in my head, father,

There's a sair pain in my side;

And ill, O ill, am I, father,

This day for to be a bride.'

18.

'O ye maun busk this bonny bride,

And put a gay mantle on;

For she shall wed this auld French lord,

Gin she should die the morn.'

19.

Some put on the gay green robes,
And some put on the brown;
But Janet put on the scarlet robes,
To shine foremost throw the town.
20.
And some they mounted the black steed,
And some mounted the brown;
But Janet mounted the milk-white steed,
To ride foremost throw the town.
21.
'O wha will guide your horse, Janet?
O wha will guide him best?'
'O wha but Willie, my true love?
He kens I lo'e him best.'

22.
And when they cam' to Marie's kirk,
To tye the haly ban',
Fair Janet's cheek looked pale and wan,
And her colour gaed and cam'.
23.
When dinner it was past and done,
And dancing to begin,
'O we'll go take the bride's maidens,
And we'll go fill the ring.'
24.
24.[1] 'ben,' into the house.
24.[4] 'downa,' like not to.
O ben then cam' the auld French lord,

Saying, 'Bride, will ye dance with me?'
'Awa', awa', ye auld French Lord,
Your face I downa see.'

25.

O ben then cam' now Sweet Willie,
He cam' with ane advance:
'O I'll go tak' the bride's maidens,
And we'll go tak' a dance.'

26.

'I've seen ither days wi' you, Willie,
And so has mony mae,
Ye would hae danced wi' me mysel',
Let a' my maidens gae.'

27.

O ben then cam' now Sweet Willie,
Saying, 'Bride, will ye dance wi' me?'
'Aye, by my sooth, and that I will,
Gin my back should break in three.'

28.

She had nae turned her throw the dance,
Throw the dance but thrice,
Whan she fell doun at Willie's feet,
And up did never rise.

29.

Willie's ta'en the key of his coffer,
And gi'en it to his man:
'Gae hame, and tell my mother dear
My horse he has me slain;

Bid her be kind to my young son,

For father has he nane.'

30.

The tane was buried in Marie's kirk,

And the tither in Marie's quire;

Out of the tane there grew a birk,

And the tither a bonny brier.

BROWN ADAM

THE TEXT is given from the Jamieson-Brown MS. It was first printed by Scott, with the omission of the second stanza—perhaps justifiable—and a few minor changes. He notes that he had seen a copy printed on a single sheet.

THE STORY has a remote parallel in a Danish ballad, extant in manuscripts of the sixteenth century and later, *Den afhugne Haand.* The tale is told as follows. Lutzelil, knowing the evil ways of Lawi Pederson, rejects his proffered love. Lawi vows she shall repent it, and the maiden is afraid for nine months to go to church, but goes at Easter. Lawi meets her in a wood, and repeats his offer. She begs him to do her no harm, feigns compliance, and makes an assignation in the chamber of her maids. She returns home and tells her father, who watches for Lawi. When he comes and demands admission, she denies the assignation. Lawi breaks down the door, and discovers Lutzelil's father with a drawn sword, with which he cuts off Lawi's hand.

The reason for objecting to the second stanza as here given is not so much the inadequacy of a golden hammer, or the unusual whiteness of the smith's fingers, but the rhyme in the third line.

BROWN ADAM

1.

1.[3] 'leeler,' more loyal.

O WHA woud wish the win' to blaw,

Or the green leaves fa' therewith?

Or wha wad wish a leeler love

Than Brown Adam the Smith?

2.

2.[2] 'study,' stithy, anvil.

His hammer's o' the beaten gold,

His study's o' the steel,

His fingers white are my delite,

He blows his bellows well.

3.

But they ha' banish'd him Brown Adam

Frae father and frae mither,

An' they ha' banish'd him Brown Adam

Frae sister and frae brither.

4.

4.[3] 'biggit,' built.

And they ha' banish'd Brown Adam

Frae the flow'r o' a' his kin;

An' he's biggit a bow'r i' the good green wood

Betwen his lady an' him.

5.

5.[2] 'thought lang,' thought (it) tedious; *i.e.* was bored. Cp. *Young Bekie*, 16.[4], etc.; *Johney Scot*, 6.[2], and elsewhere.

O it fell once upon a day

Brown Adam he thought lang,

An' he woud to the green wood gang,

To hunt some venison.

6.

He's ta'en his bow his arm o'er,

His bran' intill his han',

And he is to the good green wood,

As fast as he coud gang.

7.

O he's shot up, an' he's shot down,

The bird upo' the briar,

An' he's sent it hame to his lady,

Bade her be of good cheer.

8.

O he's shot up, an' he's shot down,

The bird upo' the thorn,

And sent it hame to his lady,

And hee'd be hame the morn.

9.

9.² 'forbye,' apart.

Whan he came till his lady's bow'r-door

He stood a little forbye,

And there he heard a fu' fa'se knight

Temptin' his gay lady.

10.

10.¹ 'he' is of course the false knight.

O he's ta'en out a gay gold ring,

Had cost him mony a poun':

'O grant me love for love, lady,

An' this sal be your own.'

11.

11.¹ 'loo,' love.

'I loo Brown Adam well,' she says,

'I wot sae does he me;

An' I woud na gi' Brown Adam's love

For nae fa'se knight I see.'

12.

12.² 'string': *i.e.* the top; purses were bags with a running string to draw the top together.

Out he has ta'en a purse of gold,

Was a' fu' to the string:

'Grant me but love for love, lady,

An' a' this sal be thine.'

13.

'I loo Brown Adam well,' she says,
'An' I ken sae does he me;
An' I woudna be your light leman
For mair nor ye coud gie.'

14.

Then out has he drawn his lang, lang bran',
An' he's flash'd it in her een:
'Now grant me love for love, lady,
Or thro' you this sal gang!'

15.

15.² 'lang': the MS. reads long.

'O,' sighing said that gay lady,
'Brown Adam tarrys lang!'
Then up it starts Brown Adam,
Says, 'I'm just at your han'.'

16.

16.¹ etc., 'gard,' made.

He's gard him leave his bow, his bow,
He's gard him leave his bran';
He's gard him leave a better pledge—
Four fingers o' his right han'.

WILLIE O' WINSBURY

THE TEXT is from the Campbell MSS.

THE STORY was imagined by Kinloch to possess a quasi-historical foundation: James V. of Scotland, who eventually married Madeleine, elder daughter of Francis I., having been previously betrothed 'by treaty' to Marie de Bourbon, daughter of the Duke of Vendôme, returned to Scotland in 1537. The theory is neither probable nor plausible.

WILLIE O' WINSBURY

1.

THE king he hath been a prisoner,
A prisoner lang in Spain, O,
And Willie o' the Winsbury
Has lain lang wi' his daughter at hame, O.

2.

'What aileth thee, my daughter Janet,
Ye look so pale and wan?
Have ye had any sore sickness,
Or have ye been lying wi' a man?
Or is it for me, your father dear,
And biding sae lang in Spain?'

3.

'I have not had any sore sickness,
Nor yet been lying wi' a man;
But it is for you, my father dear,
In biding sae lang in Spain.'

4.

'Cast ye off your berry-brown gown,
Stand straight upon the stone,

That I may ken ye by yere shape,

Whether ye be a maiden or none.'

5.

She's coosten off her berry-brown gown,

Stooden straight upo' yon stone;

Her apron was short, her haunches were round,

Her face it was pale and wan.

6.

'Is it to a man o' might, Janet?

Or is it to a man of fame?

Or is it to any of the rank robbers

That's lately come out o' Spain?'

7.

'It is not to a man of might,' she said,

'Nor is it to a man of fame;

But it is to William of Winsbury;

I could lye nae langer my lane.'

8.

The king's called on his merry men all,

By thirty and by three:

'Go fetch me William of Winsbury,

For hanged he shall be.'

9.

But when he cam' the king before,

He was clad o' the red silk;

His hair was like to threeds o' gold,

And his skin was as white as milk.

10.

'It is nae wonder,' said the king,

'That my daughter's love ye did win;
Had I been a woman, as I am a man,
My bedfellow ye should hae been.

11.
'Will ye marry my daughter Janet,
By the truth of thy right hand?
I'll gi'e ye gold, I'll gi'e ye money,
And I'll gi'e ye an earldom o' land.'
12.
'Yes, I'll marry yere daughter Janet,
By the truth of my right hand;
But I'll hae nane o' yer gold, I'll hae nane o' yer money,
Nor I winna hae an earldom o' land.
13.
'For I hae eighteen corn-mills
Runs all in water clear,
And there's as much corn in each o' them
As they can grind in a year.'

THE MARRIAGE OF SIR GAWAINE

THE TEXT is from the early part of the Percy Folio, and the ballad is therefore deficient. Where gaps are marked in the text with a row of asterisks, about nine stanzas are lost in each case—half a page torn out by a seventeenth-century maidservant to light a fire! Luckily we can supply the story from other versions.

THE STORY, also given in *The Weddynge of Sr Gawen and Dame Ragnell* (in the Rawlinson MS. C. 86 in the Bodleian Library), runs as follows:—

Shortly after Christmas, Arthur, riding by Tarn Wadling (still so called, but now pasture-land, in the forest of Inglewood), meets a bold baron, who challenges him to fight, unless he can win his ransom by returning on New Year's Day with an answer to the question, What does a woman most desire? Arthur relates the story to Gawaine, asks him and others for an answer to the riddle, and collects their suggestions in a book ('letters,' 24.[1]). On his way to keep his tryst with the baron, he meets an unspeakably ugly woman, who offers her assistance; if she will help him, Arthur says, she shall wed with Gawaine. She gives him the true answer, A woman will have her will. Arthur meets the baron, and after proffering the budget of answers, confronts him with the true answer. The baron exclaims against the ugly woman, whom he asserts to be his sister.

Arthur returns to his court, and tells his knights that a wife awaits one of them on the moor. Sir Lancelot, Sir Steven (who is not mentioned elsewhere in Arthurian tales), Sir Kay, Sir Bauier (probably Beduer or Bedivere), Sir Bore (Bors de Gauves), Sir Garrett (Gareth), and Sir Tristram ride forth to find her. At sight, Sir Kay, without overmuch chivalry, expresses his disgust, and the rest are unwilling to marry her. The king explains that he has promised to give her to Sir Gawaine, who, it seems, bows to Arthur's authority, and weds her. During the bridal night, she becomes a beautiful young woman. Further to test Gawaine, she gives him his choice: will he have her fair by day and foul by night, or foul by day and fair by night? Fair by night, says Gawaine. And foul to be seen of all by day? she asks. Have your way, says Gawaine, and breaks the last thread of the spell, as she forthwith explains: her step-mother had bewitched both her, to haunt the moor in ugly shape, till some knight should grant her *all* her will, and her brother, to challenge all comers to fight him or answer the riddle.

Similar tales, but with the important variation—undoubtedly indigenous in the story—that the man who saves his life by answering the riddle has himself to wed the ugly woman, are told by Gower (*Confessio Amantis*, Book I.) and Chaucer (*The Tale of the Wyf of Bathe*). The latter, which is also Arthurian in its setting, was made into a ballad in the *Crown Garland of Golden Roses* (*circ.* 1600), compiled by Richard Johnson. A parallel is also to be found in an Icelandic saga.

THE MARRIAGE OF SIR GAWAINE

1.

1.⁴ 'blee,' complexion.

KINGE ARTHUR liues in merry Carleile,

& seemely is to see,

& there he hath with him Queene Genever,

That bride soe bright of blee.

2.

2.⁴ Perhaps we should read 'stiff in stowre,' a constant expression in ballads, 'sturdy in fight.'

And there he hath with [him] Queene Genever,

That bride soe bright in bower,

& all his barons about him stoode,

That were both stiffe and stowre.

3.

The king kept a royall Christmasse,

Of mirth and great honor,

And when   .   .   .

  . . . . .

   * * * * *

4.

'And bring me word what thing it is

That a woman [will] most desire;

This shalbe thy ransome, Arthur,' he sayes,

'For I'le haue noe other hier.'

5.
King Arthur then held vp his hand,
According thene as was the law;
He tooke his leaue of the baron there,
& homward can he draw.

6.
And when he came to merry Carlile,
To his chamber he is gone,
& ther came to him his cozen Sir Gawaine
As he did make his mone.

7.
And there came to him his cozen Sir Gawaine
That was a curteous knight;
'Why sigh you soe sore, vnckle Arthur,' he said,
'Or who hath done thee vnright?'

8.
'O peace, O peace, thou gentle Gawaine,
That faire may thee beffall!
For if thou knew my sighing soe deepe,
Thou wold not meruaile att all;

9.
'Ffor when I came to Tearne Wadling,
A bold barron there I fand,
With a great club vpon his backe,
Standing stiffe and strong;

10.
'And he asked me wether I wold fight,
Or from him I shold begone,

Or else I must him a ransome pay

& soe depart him from.

11.

11. Arthur's customary bravery and chivalry are not conspicuous in this ballad.

'To fight with him I saw noe cause,

Methought it was not meet,

For he was stiffe & strong with-all,

His strokes were nothing sweete;

12.

'Therefor this is my ransome, Gawaine,

I ought to him to pay:

I must come againe, as I am sworne,

Vpon the Newyeer's day.

13.

'And I must bring him word what thing it is

. . . . .

. . . . .

. . . . .

* * * * *

14.

Then King Arthur drest him for to ryde

In one soe rich array

Toward the fore-said Tearne Wadling,

That he might keepe his day.

15.

And as he rode over a more,

Hee see a lady where shee sate

Betwixt an oke & a greene hollen;

She was cladd in red scarlett.

16.

Then there as shold haue stood her mouth,

Then there was sett her eye,

The other was in her forhead fast

The way that she might see.

17.

Her nose was crooked & turnd outward,

Her mouth stood foule a-wry;

A worse formed lady than shee was,

Neuer man saw with his eye.

18.

18.[1] 'halch upon,' salute.

To halch vpon him, King Arthur,

This lady was full faine,

But King Arthur had forgott his lesson,

What he shold say againe.

19.

'What knight art thou,' the lady sayd,

'That will not speak to me?

Of me be thou nothing dismayd

Tho' I be vgly to see;

20.

'For I haue halched you curteouslye,

& you will not me againe;

Yett I may happen, Sir Knight,' shee said,

'To ease thee of thy paine.'

21.

21.[1] 'Giue,' If.

'Giue thou ease me, lady,' he said,

'Or helpe me any thing,

Thou shalt have gentle Gawaine, my cozen,

& marry him with a ring.'

22.

'Why, if I help thee not, thou noble King Arthur,

Of thy owne heart's desiringe,

Of gentle Gawaine . . .

. . . . .

* * * * *

23.

And when he came to the Tearne Wadling

The baron there cold he finde,

With a great weapon on his backe,

Standing stiffe and stronge.

24.

And then he tooke King Arthur's letters in his hands,

& away he cold them fling,

& then he puld out a good browne sword,

& cryd himselfe a king.

25.

And he sayd, 'I haue thee & thy land, Arthur,

To doe as it pleaseth me,

For this is not thy ransome sure,

Therfore yeeld thee to me.'

26.

And then bespoke him noble Arthur,

& bad him hold his hand;
'& giue me leaue to speake my mind
In defence of all my land.'

27.

27.[3] 'hollen,' holly.

He said, 'As I came over a more,
I see a lady where shee sate
Betweene an oke & a green hollen;
She was clad in red scarlett;

28.

28.[3] 'sckill,' reason, judgment.

'And she says a woman will haue her will,
& this is all her cheef desire:
Doe me right, as thou art a baron of sckill,
This is thy ransome & all thy hyer.'

29.

He sayes, 'An early vengeance light on her!
She walkes on yonder more;
It was my sister that told thee this;
& she is a misshappen hore!

30.

'But heer He make mine avow to God
To doe her an euill turne,
For an euer I may thate fowle theefe get,
In a fyer I will her burne.'

* * * * *

The 2d Part

31.

Sir Lancelott & Sir Steven bold

They rode with them that day,

And the formost of the company

There rode the steward Kay.

32.

Soe did Sir Bauier and Sir Bore,

Sir Garrett with them soe gay,

Soe did Sir Tristeram that gentle knight,

To the forrest fresh & gay.

33.

And when he came to the greene fforrest,

Vnderneath a greene holly tree

Their sate that lady in red scarlet

That vnseemly was to see.

34.

34.[2] 'swire,' neck: the Folio reads *smire*.

Sir Kay beheld this ladys face,

& looked vppon her swire;

'Whosoeuer kisses this lady,' he sayes,

'Of his kisse he stands in feare.'

35.

Sir Kay beheld the lady againe,

& looked vpon her snout;

'Whosoeuer kisses this lady,' he saies,

'Of his kisse he stands in doubt.'

36.

'Peace, cozen Kay,' then said Sir Gawaine,

'Amend thee of thy life;

For there is a knight amongst vs all

That must marry her to his wife.'

37.

37.⁴ 'slaine': the Folio gives *shaine*.

'What! wedd her to wiffe!' then said Sir Kay,

'In the diuells name, anon!

Gett me a wiffe whereere I may,

For I had rather be slaine!'

38.

Then some tooke vp their hawkes in hast,

& some tooke vp their hounds,

& some sware they wold not marry her

For citty nor for towne.

39.

And then bespake him noble King Arthur,

& sware there by this day:

'For a litle foule sight & misliking

    .   .   .   .   .
    *   *   *   *   *

40.

Then shee said, 'Choose thee, gentle Gawaine,

Truth as I doe say,

Wether thou wilt haue me in this liknesse

In the night or else in the day.'

41.

41.² 'was' (Child's suggestion): the Folio reads *with*.

And then bespake him gentle Gawaine,

Was one soe mild of moode,

Sayes, 'Well I know what I wold say,

God grant it may be good!

42.

'To haue thee fowle in the night

When I with thee shold play;

Yet I had rather, if I might,

Haue thee fowle in the day.'

43.

43.[1] 'feires,' = feres, mates: the Folio reads *seires*.

'What! when Lords goe with ther feires,' shee said,

'Both to the ale & wine?

Alas! then I must hyde my selfe,

I must not goe withinne.'

44.

44.[2] Folio: *but a skill*: see note on 28.[3].

And then bespake him gentle Gawaine;

Said, 'Lady, thats but skill;

And because thou art my owne lady,

Thou shalt haue all thy will.'

45.

Then she said, 'Blessed be thou, gentle Gawaine,

This day that I thee see,

For as thou see[st] me att this time,

From hencforth I wil be:

46.

'My father was an old knight,

& yett it chanced soe

That he marryed a younge lady

That brought me to this woe.

47.

'Shee witched me, being a faire young lady,

To the greene forrest to dwell,

& there I must walke in womans likness,

Most like a feend of hell.

48.

48.[1] 'carlish,' churlish.

'She witched my brother to a carlish
b   .   .   .   .   .

  .   .   .   .   .

  .   .   .   .   .

  *   *   *   *   *

49.

  .   .   .   .

  .   .   .   .

That looked soe foule, & that was wont

On the wild more to goe.

50.

'Come kisse her, brother Kay,' then said Sir Gawaine,

'& amend thé of thy liffe;

I sweare this is the same lady

That I marryed to my wiffe.'

51.

Sir Kay kissed that lady bright,

Standing vpon his ffeete;

He swore, as he was trew knight,

The spice was neuer soe sweete.

52.

'Well, cozen Gawaine,' sayes Sir Kay,

'Thy chance is fallen arright,

For thou hast gotten one of the fairest maids

I euer saw with my sight.'

53.

'It is my fortune,' said Sir Gawaine;

'For my Vnckle Arthur's sake

I am glad as grasse wold be of raine,

Great ioy that I may take.'

54.

Sir Gawaine tooke the lady by the one arme,

Sir Kay tooke her by the tother,

They led her straight to King Arthur

As they were brother & brother.

55.

King Arthur welcomed them there all,

& soe did lady Geneuer his queene,

With all the knights of the round table

Most seemly to be seene.

56.

King Arthur beheld that lady faire

That was soe faire and bright,

He thanked Christ in Trinity

For Sir Gawaine that gentle knight;

57.

Soe did the knights, both more and lesse;

Reioyced all that day

For the good chance that hapened was

To Sir Gawaine & his lady gay.

THE BOY AND THE MANTLE

TEXT.—The Percy Folio is the sole authority for this excellent lively ballad. It is here given as it stands in the manuscript, except for division into stanzas. Percy printed the ballad *'verbatim,'*—that is, with emendations—and also a revised version.

THE STORY, which exists in countless variations in many lands, is told from the earliest times in connection with the Arthurian legend-cycle. Restricting the article used as a criterion of chastity to a mantle, we find the elements of this ballad existing in French manuscripts of the thirteenth century (the romance called *Cort Mantel*); in a Norse translation of this 'fabliau'; in the Icelandic *Mantle Rhymes* of the fifteenth century; in the *Scalachronica* of Sir Thomas Gray of Heton (*circ.* 1355); in Germany, and in Gaelic (a ballad known in Irish writings, but not in Scottish); as well as in many other versions.

The trial by the drinking-horn is a fable equally old, as far as the evidence goes, and equally widespread; but it is not told elsewhere in connection with the parallel story of the mantle. Other tests used for the purpose of discovering infidelity or unchastity are:— a crown, a magic bridge (German); a girdle (English; cp. Florimel's girdle in the *Faery Queen*, Book iv. Canto 5); a bed, a stepping-stone by the bedside, a chair (Scandinavian); flowers (Sanskrit); a shirt (German and Flemish); a picture (Italian, translated to England—cp. Massinger's *The Picture* (1630), where he localises the story in Hungary); a ring (French); a mirror (German, French, and Italian); and so forth.

Caxton, in his preface to *Kyng Arthur* (1485), says:— 'Item, in the castel of Douer ye may see Gauwayn's skull and Cradok's mantel.' Sir Thomas Gray says the mantle was made into a chasuble, and was preserved at Glastonbury.

Thomas Love Peacock says (*The Misfortunes of Elphin*, chap. xii.), 'Tegau Eurvron, or Tegau of the Golden Bosom, was the wife of Caradoc [Craddocke], and one of the Three Chaste Wives of the island of Britain.' A similar statement is recorded by Percy at the end of his 'revised and altered' ballad, taking it from 'the Rev. Evan Evans, editor of the Specimens of Welsh Poetry.'

THE BOY AND THE MANTLE

    1.

    IN the third day of May

to Carleile did come
A kind curteous child
that cold much of wisdome.

2.

2.³ 'brauches,' brooches.

A kirtle & a mantle
this child had vppon,
With brauches and ringes
full richelye bedone.

3.

He had a sute of silke,
about his middle drawne;
Without he cold of curtesye,
he thought itt much shame.

4.

'God speed thee, King Arthur,
sitting at thy meate!
& the goodly Queene Gueneuer!
I canott her fforgett.

5.

5.² 'hett,' bid; 'heede,' MS. heate.

'I tell you lords in this hall,
I hett you all heede,
Except you be the more surer,
is you for to dread.'

6.

6.¹ 'potewer.' Child says:— Read potener, French *pautonnière*, pouch, purse.

He plucked out of his potewer,

& longer wold not dwell,

He pulled forth a pretty mantle,

betweene two nut-shells.

7.

'Haue thou here, King Arthure,

haue thou heere of mee;

Give itt to thy comely queene,

shapen as itt is alreadye.

8.

8.[4] Perhaps the line should end with 'his,' but 'wiffe' is the last word in the manuscript.

'Itt shall neuer become that wiffe

that hath once done amisse':

Then euery knight in the King's court

began to care for his wiffe.

9.

9.[3] 'new-fangle,' desirous of novelties.

Forth came dame Gueneuer,

to the mantle shee her bid;

The ladye shee was new-fangle,

but yett shee was affrayd.

10.

When shee had taken the mantle,

shee stoode as she had beene madd;

It was ffrom the top to the toe

as sheeres had itt shread.

11.

11.[1] 'gaule,' perhaps = gules, *i.e.* red.

11.[3] 'wadded,' woad-coloured, *i.e.* blue.

One while was itt gaule,

another while was itt greene;

Another while was itt wadded;

ill itt did her beseeme.

12.

Another while was it blacke,

& bore the worst hue;

'By my troth,' quoth King Arthur,

'I thinke thou be not true.'

13.

13.[2] 'blee,' colour.

13.[3] 'rudd,' complexion.

Shee threw downe the mantle,

that bright was of blee,

Fast with a rudd redd

to her chamber can shee flee.

14.

14.[1] 'walker,' fuller.

Shee curst the weauer and the walker

that clothe that had wrought,

& bade a vengeance on his crowne

that hither hath itt brought.

15.

'I had rather be in a wood,

vnder a greene tree,

Then in King Arthurs court,

shamed for to bee.'

16.

Kay called forth his ladye,

& bade her come neere;

Saies, 'Madam, & thou be guiltye,

I pray thee hold thee there.'

17.

Forth came his ladye

shortlye and anon,

Boldlye to the mantle

then is shee gone.

18.

When shee had tane the mantle,

& cast it her about,

Then was shee bare

all aboue the buttocckes.

19.

Then euery knight

that was in the Kings court

Talked, laug[h]ed, & showted,

full oft att that sport.

20.

Shee threw downe the mantle,

that bright was of blee,

Ffast with a red rudd

to her chamber can shee flee.

21.

Forth came an old knight,

pattering ore a creede,

& he proferred to this litle boy

20 markes to his meede,

22.
& all the time of the Christmasse
willinglye to ffeede;
For why this mantle might
doe his wiffe some need.

23.
When shee had tane the mantle,
of cloth that was made,
Shee had no more left on her
but a tassell and a threed:
Then euery knight in the Kings court
bade euill might shee speed.
24.
She threw downe the mantle,
that bright was of blee,
& fast with a redd rudd
to her chamber can shee flee.
25.
25.[4] 'dinne,' trouble.
Craddocke called forth his ladye,
& bade her come in;
Saith, 'Winne this mantle, ladye,
with a litle dinne.
26.
'Winne this mantle, ladye,
& it shalbe thine
If thou neuer did amisse
since thou wast mine.'

27.
Forth came Craddockes ladye
shortlye & anon,
But boldlye to the mantle
then is shee gone.
28.
28.[4] 'crowt,' pucker.
When shee had tane the mantle,
& cast itt her about,
Vpp att her great toe
itt began to crinkle & crowt;
Shee said, 'Bowe downe, mantle,
& shame me not for nought.

29.
'Once I did amisse,
I tell you certainlye,
When I kist Craddockes mouth
vnder a greene tree,
When I kist Craddockes mouth
before he marryed mee.'
30.
When shee had her shreeuen,
& her sines shee had tolde,
The mantle stoode about her
right as shee wold,
31.
Seemelye of coulour,
glittering like gold;

Then euery knight in Arthurs court
did her behold.
32.
Then spake dame Gueneuer
to Arthur our king:
'She hath tane yonder mantle,
not with wright but with wronge.
33.
'See you not yonder woman
that maketh her selfe soe cleane?
I haue seene tane out of her bedd
of men fiueteene;
34.
34.[2] 'by-deene,' one after another.
'Preists, clarkes, & wedded men,
from her by-deene;
Yett shee taketh the mantle,
& maketh her selfe cleane!'

35.
Then spake the litle boy
that kept the mantle in hold;
Sayes, 'King, chasten thy wiffe;
of her words shee is to bold.
36.
'Shee is a bitch & a witch,
& a whore bold;
King, in thine owne hall
thou art a cuchold.'

37.

37 and 38: Evidently some lines have been lost here, and the rhymes are thereby confused.

A litle boy stoode

looking ouer a dore;

He was ware of a wyld bore,

wold haue werryed a man.

38.

He pulld forth a wood kniffe,

fast thither that he ran;

He brought in the bores head,

& quitted him like a man.

39.

He brought in the bores head,

and was wonderous bold;

He said there was neuer a cucholds kniffe

carue itt that cold.

40.

Some rubbed their k[n]iues

vppon a whetstone;

Some threw them vnder the table,

& said they had none.

41.

King Arthur & the child

stood looking them vpon;

All their k[n]iues edges

turned backe againe.

42.

42.[3] 'birtled,' cut up.

Craddoccke had a litle kniue
of iron & of steele;
He birtled the bores head
wonderous weele,
That euery knight in the Kings court
had a morssell.

43.

43.[2] 'ronge,' rang.

The litle boy had a horne,
of red gold that ronge;
He said, 'There was noe cuckolde
shall drinke of my horne,
But he shold itt sheede,
either behind or beforne.'

44.

Some shedd on their shoulder,
& some on their knee;
He that cold not hitt his mouth
put it in his eye;
& he that was a cuckold,
euery man might him see.

45.

Craddoccke wan the horne
& the bores head;
His ladye wan the mantle
vnto her meede;
Euerye such a louely ladye,
God send her well to speede!

JOHNEY SCOT

THE TEXT of this popular and excellent ballad is given from the Jamieson-Brown MS. It was copied, with wilful alterations, into Scott's Abbotsford MS. called *Scottish Songs*. Professor Child prints sixteen variants of the ballad, nearly all from manuscripts.

THE STORY of the duel with the Italian is given with more detail in other versions. In two ballads from Motherwell's MS., where 'the Italian' becomes 'the Tailliant' or 'the Talliant,' the champion jumps over Johney's head, and descends on the point of Johney's sword. This exploit is paralleled in a Breton ballad, where the Seigneur Les Aubrays of St. Brieux is ordered by the French king to combat his wild Moor, who leaps in the air and is received on the sword of his antagonist. Again, in Scottish tradition, James Macgill, having killed Sir Robert Balfour about 1679, went to London to procure his pardon, which Charles II. offered him on the condition of fighting an Italian gladiator. The Italian leaped once over James Macgill, but in attempting to repeat this manœuvre was spitted by his opponent, who thereby procured not only his pardon, but also knighthood.

JOHNEY SCOT

1.

O JOHNEY was as brave a knight

As ever sail'd the sea,

An' he's done him to the English court,

To serve for meat and fee.

2.

He had nae been in fair England

But yet a little while,

Untill the kingis ae daughter

To Johney proves wi' chil'.

3.

O word's come to the king himsel',

In his chair where he sat,

That his ae daughter was wi' bairn

To Jack, the Little Scott.

4.

'Gin this be true that I do hear,

As I trust well it be,

Ye pit her into prison strong,

An' starve her till she die.'

5.

5.2,4 'A wot' = I wis.

O Johney's on to fair Scotland,

A wot he went wi' speed,

An' he has left the kingis court,

A wot good was his need.

6.

6.2 See *Young Bekie*, 16.4; *Brown Adam*, 5.2.

O it fell once upon a day

That Johney he thought lang,

An' he's gane to the good green wood,

As fast as he coud gang.

7.

'O whare will I get a bonny boy,

To rin my errand soon,

That will rin into fair England,

An' haste him back again?'

8.

O up it starts a bonny boy,

Gold yallow was his hair,

I wish his mother meickle joy,

His bonny love mieckle mair.

9.

'O here am I, a bonny boy,

Will rin your errand soon;

I will gang into fair England,

An' come right soon again.'

10.

10. See *Lady Maisry*, 21; *Lord Ingram and Chiel Wyet*, 12, etc.: a stock ballad-phrase.

O whan he came to broken briggs,

He bent his bow and swam;

An' whan he came to the green grass growan,

He slaikid his shoone an' ran.

11.

Whan he came to yon high castèl,

He ran it roun' about,

An' there he saw the king's daughter,

At the window looking out.

12.

12.[1] 'sark,' shift.

12.[4] 'Speer' (speir), ask.

'O here's a sark o' silk, lady,

Your ain han' sew'd the sleeve;

You'r bidden come to fair Scotlan',

Speer nane o' your parents' leave.

13.

13.[2] 'gare,' gore: see *Brown Robin*, 10.[4].

'Ha, take this sark o' silk, lady,

Your ain han' sew'd the gare;

- 170 -

You're bidden come to good green wood,

Love Johney waits you there.'

14.

She's turn'd her right and roun' about,

The tear was in her ee:

'How can I come to my true-love,

Except I had wings to flee?

15.

'Here am I kept wi' bars and bolts,

Most grievous to behold;

My breast-plate's o' the sturdy steel,

Instead of the beaten gold.

16.

'But tak' this purse, my bonny boy,

Ye well deserve a fee,

An' bear this letter to my love,

An' tell him what you see.'

17.

Then quickly ran the bonny boy

Again to Scotlan' fair,

An' soon he reach'd Pitnachton's tow'rs,

An' soon found Johney there.

18.

18.[4] 'loote,' let.

He pat the letter in his han'

An' taul' him what he sa',

But eer he half the letter read,

He loote the tears doun fa'.

19.

'O I will gae back to fair Englan',
Tho' death shoud me betide,
An' I will relieve the damesel
That lay last by my side.'

20.
Then out it spake his father dear,
'My son, you are to blame;
An' gin you'r catch'd on English groun',
I fear you'll ne'er win hame.'
21.
Then out it spake a valiant knight,
Johny's best friend was he;
'I can commaun' five hunder men,
An' I'll his surety be.'
22.
22.4 'mess,' mass.
The firstin town that they came till,
They gard the bells be rung;
An' the nextin town that they came till,
They gard the mess be sung.
23.
The thirdin town that they came till,
They gard the drums beat roun';
The king but an' his nobles a'
Was startl'd at the soun'.
24.
Whan they came to the king's palace
They rade it roun' about,

An' there they saw the king himsel',

At the window looking out.

25.

'Is this the Duke o' Albany,

Or James, the Scottish king?

Or are ye some great foreign lord,

That's come a visiting?'

26.

'I'm nae the Duke of Albany,

Nor James, the Scottish king;

But I'm a valiant Scottish knight,

Pitnachton is my name.'

27.

27.[3] 'or,' ere.

'O if Pitnachton be your name,

As I trust well it be,

The morn, or I tast meat or drink,

You shall be hanged hi'.'

28.

Then out it spake the valiant knight

That came brave Johney wi';

'Behold five hunder bowmen bold,

Will die to set him free.'

29.

29.[2] The second 'laugh' is the past tense of the verb.

Then out it spake the king again,

An' a scornfu' laugh laugh he;

'I have an Italian in my house

Will fight you three by three.'

30.

'O grant me a boon,' brave Johney cried;

'Bring your Italian here;

Then if he fall beneath my sword,

I've won your daughter dear.'

31.

31.² 'gurious,' grim, ugly.

Then out it came that Italian,

An' a gurious ghost was he;

Upo' the point o' Johney's sword

This Italian did die.

32.

Out has he drawn his lang, lang bran',

Struck it across the plain:

'Is there any more o' your English dogs

That you want to be slain?'

33.

33.² 'tocher,' dowry.

'A clark, a clark,' the king then cried,

'To write her tocher free';

'A priest, a priest,' says Love Johney,

'To marry my love and me.

34.

'I'm seeking nane o' your gold,' he says,

'Nor of your silver clear;

I only seek your daughter fair,

Whose love has cost her dear.'

LORD INGRAM AND CHIEL WYET

THE TEXT is taken from Motherwell's *Minstrelsy*, a similar version being given in Maidment's *North Countrie Garland*. A few alterations from the latter version are incorporated.

THE STORY bears tokens of confusion with *Lady Maisry* in some of the variants of either, but here the tragedy is that the bridegroom is brother to the lover. The end of this ballad in all its forms is highly unnatural in its style: why should Maisery's remorse at having been such an expense to Lord Ingram be three times as great as her grief for the loss of her lover? It is by no means romantic.

LORD INGRAM AND CHIEL WYET

1.

1.4 'honour': Motherwell printed *bonheur*.

LORD INGRAM and Chiel Wyet

Was baith born in one bower;

Laid baith their hearts on one lady,

The less was their honour.

2.

Chiel Wyet and Lord Ingram

Was baith born in one hall;

Laid baith their hearts on one lady,

The worse did them befall.

3.

Lord Ingram woo'd her Lady Maisery

From father and from mother;

Lord Ingram woo'd her Lady Maisery

From sister and from brother.

4.

Lord Ingram woo'd her Lady Maisery

With leave of a' her kin;

And every one gave full consent,

But she said no to him.

5.

Lord Ingram woo'd her Lady Maisery

Into her father's ha';

Chiel Wyet woo'd her Lady Maisery

Amang the sheets so sma'.

6.

6.³ 'ben,' in.

Now it fell out upon a day

She was dressing her head,

That ben did come her father dear,

Wearing the gold so red.

7.

He said, 'Get up now, Lady Maisery,

Put on your wedding gown;

For Lord Ingram he will be here,

Your wedding must be done.'

8.

8.² 'sell': Motherwell gave *kill*.

'I'd rather be Chiel Wyet's wife,

The white fish for to sell,

Before I were Lord Ingram's wife,

To wear the silk so well.

9.

'I'd rather be Chiel Wyet's wife,

With him to beg my bread,

Before I were Lord Ingram's wife,

To wear the gold so red.

10.
'Where will I get a bonny boy,
Will win gold to his fee,
And will run unto Chiel Wyet's,
With this letter from me?'

11.
'O here I am, the boy,' says one,
'Will win gold to my fee,
And carry away any letter
To Chiel Wyet from thee.'

12.

12. Cp. *Lady Maisry*, 21.

And when he found the bridges broke
He bent his bow and swam;
And when he found the grass growing,
He hastened and he ran.

13.
And when he came to Chiel Wyet's castle,
He did not knock nor call,
But set his bent bow to his breast,
And lightly leaped the wall;
And ere the porter open'd the gate,
The boy was in the hall.

14.
The first line he looked on,
A grieved man was he;
The next line he looked on,

A tear blinded his ee:

Says, 'I wonder what ails my one brother,

He'll not let my love be!

15.

'But I'll send to my brother's bridal—

The bacon shall be mine—

Full four and twenty buck and roe,

And ten tun of the wine;

And bid my love be blythe and glad,

And I will follow syne.'

16.

16.4 'neen,' none, not.

There was not a groom about that castle,

But got a gown of green,

And all was blythe, and all was glad,

But Lady Maisery she was neen.

17.

There was no cook about that kitchen,

But got a gown of gray;

And all was blythe, and all was glad,

But Lady Maisery was wae.

18.

18.2 'garl,' gravel.

Between Mary Kirk and that castle

Was all spread ower with garl,

To keep Lady Maisery and her maidens

From tramping on the marl.

19.

From Mary Kirk to that castle

Was spread a cloth of gold,

To keep Lady Maisery and her maidens

From treading on the mold.

20.

When mass was sung, and bells was rung,

And all men bound for bed;

Then Lord Ingram and Lady Maisery

In one bed they were laid.

21.

When they were laid into their bed,

It was baith saft and warm,

He laid his hand over her side,

Says, 'I think you are with bairn.'

22.

'I told you once, so did I twice,

When ye came me to woo,

That Chiel Wyet, your only brother,

One night lay in my bower.

23.

'I told you twice, I told you thrice,

Ere ye came me to wed,

That Chiel Wyet, your one brother,

One night lay in my bed.'

24.

'O will you father your bairn on me,

And on no other man?

And I'll give him to his dowry

Full fifty ploughs of land.'

25.

'I will not father my bairn on you,
Nor on no wrongeous man,
Though ye would give him to his dowry
Five thousand ploughs of land.'

26.

26.¹ Motherwell gives *did stand*.
Then up did start him Chiel Wyet,
Shed by his yellow hair,
And gave Lord Ingram to the heart
A deep wound and a sair.

27.

Then up did start him Lord Ingram,
Shed by his yellow hair,
And gave Chiel Wyet to the heart,
A deep wound and a sair.

28.

28.⁴ 'brain,' mad.
There was no pity for that two lords,
Where they were lying slain;
But all was for her Lady Maisery,
In that bower she gaed brain.

29.

There was no pity for that two lords,
When they were lying dead;
But all was for her Lady Maisery,
In that bower she went mad.

30.

30.² 'tree,' wood.

Said, 'Get to me a cloak of cloth,

A staff of good hard tree;

If I have been an evil woman,

I shall beg till I dee.

31.

31.¹ 'a' = ae, each.

'For a bit I'll beg for Chiel Wyet,

For Lord Ingram I'll beg three;

All for the good and honourable marriage,

At Mary Kirk he gave me.'

THE TWA SISTERS O' BINNORIE

TEXTS.—The version here given is compounded from two different sources, almost of necessity. Stanzas 1-19 were given by Scott, compounded from W. Tytler's Brown MS. and the recitation of an old woman. But at stanza 20 Scott's version becomes eccentric, and he prints such verses as:—

'A famous harper passing by

The sweet pale face he chanced to spy . . .

The strings he framed of her yellow hair,

Whose notes made sad the listening air.'

Stanzas 20-25, therefore, have been supplied from the Jamieson-Brown MS., which after this point does not descend from the high level of ballad-poetry.

THE STORY.—This is a very old and a very popular story. An early broadside exists, dated 1656, and the same version is printed in *Wit Restor'd*, 1658. Of Scandinavian ballads on the same subject, nine are Danish, two Icelandic, twelve Norwegian, four Färöe, and eight or nine Swedish.

THE TWA SISTERS O' BINNORIE

1.

THERE were twa sisters sat in a bour,

Binnorie, O Binnorie!

There came a knight to be their wooer,

By the bonny mill-dams o' Binnorie.

2.

He courted the eldest wi' glove and ring,

Binnorie, O Binnorie!

But he lo'ed the youngest aboon a' thing,

By the bonny mill-dams o' Binnorie.

3.

He courted the eldest with broach and knife,
Binnorie, O Binnorie!
But he lo'ed the youngest aboon his life,
By the bonny mill-dams o' Binnorie.
4.
The eldest she was vexed sair,
Binnorie, O Binnorie!
And sair envìed her sister fair,
By the bonny mill-dams o' Binnorie.
5.
The eldest said to the youngest ane,
Binnorie, O Binnorie!
'Will ye go and see our father's ships come in?'
By the bonny mill-dams o' Binnorie.
6.
She's ta'en her by the lilly hand,
Binnorie, O Binnorie!
And led her down to the river-strand,
By the bonny mill-dams o' Binnorie.
7.
The youngest stude upon a stane,
Binnorie, O Binnorie!
The eldest came and pushed her in,
By the bonny mill-dams o' Binnorie.
8.
8.[3] 'jaw,' wave.
She took her by the middle sma',
Binnorie, O Binnorie!

And dashed her bonnie back to the jaw,
By the bonny mill-dams o' Binnorie/
9.
'O sister, sister, reach your hand!'
Binnorie, O Binnorie!
'And ye shall be heir of half my land,'
By the bonny mill-dams o' Binnorie.
10.
'O sister, I'll not reach my hand,'
Binnorie, O Binnorie!
'And I'll be heir of all your land,'
By the bonny mill-dams o' Binnorie.
11.
11.[3] 'my world's make,' my earthly mate.
'Shame fa' the hand that I should take,'
Binnorie, O Binnorie!
'It's twin'd me and my world's make,'
By the bonny mill-dams o' Binnorie.
12.
'O sister, reach me but your glove,'
Binnorie, O Binnorie!
'And sweet William shall be your love,'
By the bonny mill-dams o' Binnorie.
13.
'Sink on, nor hope for hand or glove,'
Binnorie, O Binnorie!
'And sweet William shall better be my love,'
By the bonny mill-dams o' Binnorie.
14.

'Your cherry cheeks and your yellow hair,'
Binnorie, O Binnorie!
'Garr'd me gang maiden evermair,'
By the bonnie mill-dams o' Binnorie.

15.
Sometimes she sunk, and sometimes she swam,
Binnorie, O Binnorie!
Until she came to the miller's dam,
By the bonny mill-dams o' Binnorie.
16.
'O father, father, draw your dam!'
Binnorie, O Binnorie!
'There's either a mermaid or a milk-white swan,'
By the bonny mill-dams o' Binnorie.
17.
The miller hasted and drew his dam,
Binnorie, O Binnorie!
And there he found a drowned woman,
By the bonny mill-dams o' Binnorie.
18.
You could not see her yellow hair,
Binnorie, O Binnorie!
For gowd and pearls that were sae rare,
By the bonny mill-dams o' Binnorie.
19.
You could na see her middle sma',
Binnorie, O Binnorie!
Her gowden girdle was sae bra',

By the bonny mill-dams o' Binnorie.

20.

An' by there came a harper fine,
Binnorie, O Binnorie!
That harped to the king at dine,
By the bonny mill-dams o' Binnorie.

21.

When he did look that lady upon,
Binnorie, O Binnorie!
He sigh'd and made a heavy moan,
By the bonny mill-dams o' Binnorie.

22.

He's ta'en three locks o' her yallow hair,
Binnorie, O Binnorie!
And wi' them strung his harp sae fair,
By the bonny mill-dams o' Binnorie.

23.

The first tune he did play and sing,
Binnorie, O Binnorie!
Was, 'Farewell to my father the king,'
By the bonny mill-dams o' Binnorie.

24.

The nextin tune that he play'd syne,
Binnorie, O Binnorie!

Was, 'Farewell to my mother the queen,'
By the bonny mill-dams o' Binnorie.
25.
The lasten tune that he play'd then,
Binnorie, O Binnorie!
Was, 'Wae to my sister, fair Ellen!'
By the bonny mill-dams o' Binnorie.

YOUNG WATERS

THE TEXT is that of a copy mentioned by Percy, 'printed not long since at Glasgow, in one sheet 8vo. The world was indebted for its publication to the lady Jean Hume, sister to the Earle of Hume, who died lately at Gibraltar.' The original edition, discovered by Mr. Macmath after Professor Child's version (from the *Reliques*) was in print, is:— 'Young Waters, an Ancient Scottish Poem, never before printed. Glasgow, printed and sold by Robert and Andrew Foulis, 1755.' This was also known to Maidment. Hardly a word differs from Percy's version; but here I have substituted the spellings 'wh' for Percy's 'quh,' in 'quhen,' etc., and 'y' for his 'z' in 'zoung, zou,' etc.

THE STORY has had historical foundations suggested for it by Percy and Chambers. Percy identified Young Waters with the Earl of Murray, murdered, according to the chronicle of Sir James Balfour, on the 7th of February 1592. Chambers, in 1829, relying on Buchan's version of the ballad, had no doubt that Young Waters was one of the Scots nobles executed by James I., and was very probably Walter Stuart, second son of the Duke of Albany. Thirty years later, Chambers was equally certain that the ballad was the composition of Lady Wardlaw.

In a Scandinavian ballad, Folke Lovmandson is a favourite at court; a little wee page makes the fatal remark and excites the king's jealousy. The innocent knight is rolled down a hill in a barrel set with knives—a punishment common in Scandinavian folklore.

YOUNG WATERS

1.

1.[2] 'round tables,' an unknown game.

ABOUT Yule, when the wind blew cule,

And the round tables began,

A there is cum to our king's court

Mony a well-favor'd man.

2.

The queen luikt owre the castle-wa',

Beheld baith dale and down,

And there she saw Young Waters
Cum riding to the town.

3.

His footmen they did rin before,
His horsemen rade behind;
Ane mantel of the burning gowd
Did keip him frae the wind.

4.

4.¹ 'graith'd,' harnessed, usually; here perhaps shod.

Gowden-graith'd his horse before,
And siller-shod behind;
The horse Young Waters rade upon
Was fleeter than the wind.

5.

Out then spack a wylie lord,
Unto the queen said he:
'O tell me wha 's the fairest face
Rides in the company?'

6.

6.¹ 'laird,' a landholder, below the degree of knight.—JAMIESON.

'I've sene lord, and I've sene laird,
And knights of high degree,
Bot a fairer face than Young Waters
Mine eyne did never see.'

7.

Out then spack the jealous king,
And an angry man was he:
'O if he had bin twice as fair,

You micht have excepted me.'

8.

'You're neither laird nor lord,' she says,

'Bot the king that wears the crown;

There is not a knight in fair Scotland

Bot to thee maun bow down.'

9.

For a' that she coud do or say,

Appeas'd he wad nae bee,

Bot for the words which she had said,

Young Waters he maun die.

10.

They hae ta'en Young Waters,

And put fetters to his feet;

They hae ta'en Young Waters, and

Thrown him in dungeon deep.

11.

'Aft have I ridden thro' Stirling town,

In the wind bot and the weit;

Bot I neir rade thro' Stirling town

Wi' fetters at my feet.

12.

'Aft have I ridden thro' Stirling town,

In the wind bot and the rain;

Bot I neir rade thro' Stirling town

Neir to return again.'

13.

13.[1] 'heiding-hill': *i.e.* heading (beheading) hill. The place of execution was anciently an artificial hillock.—PERCY.

They hae ta'en to the heiding-hill

His young son in his craddle,

And they hae ta'en to the heiding-hill
His horse bot and his saddle.
14.
They hae ta'en to heiding-hill
His lady fair to see,
And for the words the queen had spoke
Young Waters he did die.

BARBARA ALLAN

THE TEXT is from Allan Ramsay's *Tea-Table Miscellany* (1763). It was not included in the first edition (1724-1727), nor until the ninth edition in 1740, when to the original three volumes there was added a fourth, in which this ballad appeared. There is also a Scotch version, *Sir John Grehme and Barbara Allan*. Percy printed both in the *Reliques*, vol. iii.

THE STORY of Barbara Allan's scorn of her lover and subsequent regret has always been popular. Pepys records of Mrs. Knipp, 'In perfect pleasure I was to hear her sing, and especially her little Scotch song of Barbary Allen' (January 2, 1665-6). Goldsmith's words are equally well known: 'The music of the finest singer is dissonance to what I felt when an old dairymaid sung me into tears with *Johnny Armstrong's Last Goodnight*, or *The Cruelty of Barbara Allen*.' The tune is excessively popular: it is given in Chappell's *English Song and Ballad Music*.

BARBARA ALLAN

1.

IT was in and about the Martinmas time,

When the green leaves were afalling,

That Sir John Græme, in the West Country,

Fell in love with Barbara Allan.

2.

He sent his men down through the town,

To the place where she was dwelling;

'O haste and come to my master dear,

Gin ye be Barbara Allan.'

3.

O hooly, hooly rose she up,

To the place where he was lying,

And when she drew the curtain by,

'Young man, I think you're dying.'

4.
'O it's I am sick, and very, very sick,
And 't is a' for Barbara Allan.'
'O the better for me ye 's never be,
Tho' your heart's blood were aspilling.'
5.
'O dinna ye mind, young man,' said she,
'When ye was in the tavern a drinking,
That ye made the healths gae round and round,
And slighted Barbara Allan?'
6.
He turn'd his face unto the wall,
And death was with him dealing;
'Adieu, adieu, my dear friends all,
And be kind to Barbara Allan.'
7.
And slowly, slowly raise she up,
And slowly, slowly left him,
And sighing, said, she coud not stay,
Since death of life had reft him.
8.
She had not gane a mile but twa,
When she heard the dead-bell ringing,

And every jow that the dead-bell geid,
It cry'd, 'Woe to Barbara Allan!'

9.
'O mother, mother, make my bed,
O make it saft and narrow!
Since my love died for me to-day,
I'll die for him to-morrow.'

THE GAY GOSHAWK

THE TEXT is from the Jamieson-Brown MS., on which version Scott drew partly for his ballad in the *Minstrelsy*. Mrs. Brown recited the ballad again to William Tytler in 1783, but the result is now lost, with most of the other Tytler-Brown versions.

THE STORY.—One point, the maid's feint of death to escape from her father to her lover, is the subject of a ballad very popular in France; a version entitled *Belle Isambourg* is printed in a collection called *Airs de Cour*, 1607. Feigning death to escape various threats is a common feature in many European ballads.

It is perhaps needless to remark that no goshawk sings sweetly, much less talks. In Buchan's version (of forty-nine stanzas) the goshawk is exchanged for a parrot.

THE GAY GOSHAWK

    1.

'O WELL's me o' my gay goss-hawk,

That he can speak and flee;

He'll carry a letter to my love,

Bring back another to me.'

    2.

2.[3] 'couth,' word.—JAMIESON. The derivation, from Anglo-Saxon *cwide*, is hard.

'O how can I your true-love ken,

Or how can I her know?

When frae her mouth I never heard couth,

Nor wi' my eyes her saw.'

    3.

'O well sal ye my true-love ken,

As soon as you her see;

For, of a' the flow'rs in fair Englan',

The fairest flow'r is she.

4.

'At even at my love's bow'r-door

There grows a bowing birk,

An' sit ye down and sing thereon

As she gangs to the kirk.

5.

'An' four-and-twenty ladies fair

Will wash and go to kirk,

But well shall ye my true-love ken,

For she wears goud on her skirt.

6.

'An' four-and-twenty gay ladies

Will to the mass repair,

But well sal ye my true-love ken,

For she wears goud on her hair.'

7.

7.[3] 'she' is the goshawk; called 'he' in 1.[2].

O even at that lady's bow'r-door

There grows a bowin' birk,

An' she sat down and sang thereon,

As she ged to the kirk.

8.

8.[3] 'shot-window,' here perhaps a bow-window.

'O eet and drink, my marys a',

The wine flows you among,

Till I gang to my shot-window,

An' hear yon bonny bird's song.

9.

9.² 'streen' = yestreen, last evening.

'Sing on, sing on, my bonny bird,

The song ye sang the streen,

For I ken by your sweet singin',

You 're frae my true-love sen'.'

10.

O first he sang a merry song,

An' then he sang a grave,

An' then he peck'd his feathers gray,

To her the letter gave.

11.

'Ha, there's a letter frae your love,

He says he sent you three;

He canna wait your love langer,

But for your sake he'll die.

12.

'He bids you write a letter to him;

He says he's sent you five;

He canno wait your love langer,

Tho' you're the fairest woman alive.'

13.

'Ye bid him bake his bridal bread,

And brew his bridal ale,

An' I'll meet him in fair Scotlan'

Lang, lang or it be stale.'

14.

She's doen her to her father dear,

Fa'n low down on her knee:

'A boon, a boon, my father dear,

I pray you, grant it me.'

15.

'Ask on, ask on, my daughter,

An' granted it sal be;

Except ae squire in fair Scotlan',

An' him you sall never see.'

16.

'The only boon my father dear,

That I do crave of the,

Is, gin I die in southin lans,

In Scotland to bury me.

17.

'An' the firstin kirk that ye come till,

Ye gar the bells be rung,

An' the nextin kirk that ye come till,

Ye gar the mess be sung.

18.

'An' the thirdin kirk that ye come till,

You deal gold for my sake,

An' the fourthin kirk that ye come till,

You tarry there till night.'

19.

19.[1] 'bigly,' *lit.* habitable; the stock epithet of 'bower.'

She is doen her to her bigly bow'r,

As fast as she coud fare,

An' she has tane a sleepy draught,

That she had mix'd wi' care.

20.

She's laid her down upon her bed,

An' soon she's fa'n asleep,

And soon o'er every tender limb

Cauld death began to creep.

21.

Whan night was flown, an' day was come,

Nae ane that did her see

But thought she was as surely dead

As ony lady coud be.

22.

Her father an' her brothers dear

Gard make to her a bier;

The tae half was o' guid red gold,

The tither o' silver clear.

23.

Her mither an' her sisters fair

Gard work for her a sark;

The tae half was o' cambrick fine,

The tither o' needle wark.

24.

The firstin kirk that they came till,

They gard the bells be rung,

An' the nextin kirk that they came till,

They gard the mess be sung.

25.

25.[4] 'make,' mate, lover.

The thirdin kirk that they came till,

They dealt gold for her sake,

An' the fourthin kirk that they came till,

Lo, there they met her make!

26.

'Lay down, lay down the bigly bier,

Lat me the dead look on';

Wi' cherry cheeks and ruby lips

She lay an' smil'd on him.

27.

27.[1] 'sheave,' slice.

'O ae sheave o' your bread, true-love,

An' ae glass o' your wine,

For I hae fasted for your sake

These fully days is nine.

28.

'Gang hame, gang hame, my seven bold brothers,

Gang hame and sound your horn;

An' ye may boast in southin lan's

Your sister's play'd you scorn.'

BROWN ROBIN

THE TEXT is here given from the Jamieson-Brown MS. Versions, lengthened and therefore less succinct and natural, are given in Christie's *Traditional Ballad Airs* (*Love Robbie*) and in Buchan's *Ballads of the North of Scotland* (*Brown Robyn and Mally*).

THE STORY is a genuine bit of romance. The proud porter is apparently suspicious, believing that the king's daughter would not have made him drunk for any good purpose. In spite of that he cannot see through Brown Robin's disguise, though the king remarks that 'this is a sturdy dame.' The king's daughter, one would think, who conceals Robin's bow in her bosom, must also have been somewhat sturdy. Note the picturesque touch in 8.[2].

BROWN ROBIN

1.[2] 'birling,' drinking: cf. 7.[1].

1.

THE king but an' his nobles a' } *bis*
Sat birling at the wine;

He would ha' nane but his ae daughter

To wait on them at dine.

2.

She's served them butt, she's served them ben,

Intill a gown of green,

But her e'e was ay on Brown Robin,

That stood low under the rain.

3.

3.[1] 'bigly,' commodious: see *The Gay Goshawk*, 19.[1].

3.[3] 'shot-window,' here perhaps a shutter with a pane of glass let in.

She's doen her to her bigly bow'r,

As fast as she coud gang,

An' there she's drawn her shot-window,

An' she's harped an' she sang.

4.

'There sits a bird i' my father's garden,

An' O but she sings sweet!

I hope to live an' see the day

When wi' my love I'll meet.'

5.

'O gin that ye like me as well

As your tongue tells to me,

What hour o' the night, my lady bright,

At your bow'r sal I be?'

6.

'Whan my father an' gay Gilbert

Are baith set at the wine,

O ready, ready I will be

To lat my true-love in.'

7.

7.[1] 'birl'd,' plied: cf. 1.[2].

7.[4] Cf. *Fause Footrage* 16.[4]: a popular simile.

7.[5] 'stown,' stolen: 'yates,' gates.

O she has birl'd her father's porter

Wi' strong beer an' wi' wine,

Untill he was as beastly drunk

As ony wild-wood swine:

She's stown the keys o' her father's yates

An latten her true-love in.

8.

When night was gane, an' day was come,
An' the sun shone on their feet,
Then out it spake him Brown Robin,
'I'll be discover'd yet.'
9.
Then out it spake that gay lady:
'My love ye need na doubt,
For wi' ae wile I've got you in,
Wi' anither I'll bring you out.'
10.
10.[4] 'gare,' gore; *i.e.* by her knee: a stock ballad phrase.
She's ta'en her to her father's cellar,
As fast as she can fare;
She's drawn a cup o' the gude red wine,
Hung 't low down by her gare;
An' she met wi' her father dear
Just coming down the stair.
11.
11.[4] 'gantrees,' stands for casks.
'I woud na gi' that cup, daughter,
That ye hold i' your han',
For a' the wines in my cellar,
An' gantrees whare the[y] stan'.'
12.
12.[3] 'sic,' such: the MS. gives *sick*: 'steer,' disturbance.
'O wae be to your wine, father,
That ever 't came o'er the sea;
'Tis pitten my head in sic a steer
I' my bow'r I canna be.'

13.

13.4 'marys,' maids.

'Gang out, gang out, my daughter dear,

Gang out an' tack the air;

Gang out an' walk i' the good green wood,

An' a' your marys fair.'

14.

Then out it spake the proud porter—

Our lady wish'd him shame—

'We'll send the marys to the wood,

But we'll keep our lady at hame.'

15.

15.4 'gains for,' suits, is meet (Icelandic, *gegna*). Cf. Jamieson's version of *Sir Patrick Spence*:—
'For I brought as much white money
As will gain my men and me.'

'There's thirty marys i' my bow'r,

There's thirty o' them an' three;

But there 's nae ane amo' them a'

Kens what flow'r gains for me.'

16.

She's doen her to her bigly bow'r

As fast as she could gang,

An' she has dresst him Brown Robin

Like ony bow'r-woman.

17.

17.4 'cordwain,' Cordovan (Spanish) leather.

The gown she pat upon her love

Was o' the dainty green,

His hose was o' the saft, saft silk,

His shoon o' the cordwain fine.

18.

She's pitten his bow in her bosom,

His arrow in her sleeve,

His sturdy bran' her body next,

Because he was her love.

19.

Then she is unto her bow'r-door

As fast as she coud gang;

But out it spake the proud porter—

Our lady wish'd him shame—

'We'll count our marys to the wood,

And we'll count them back again.'

20.

The firsten mary she sent out

Was Brown Robin by name;

Then out it spake the king himsel',

'This is a sturdy dame.'

21.

21.[2] 'gay': the MS. gives *gray*. This is Child's emendation, who points out that the sun was up, 8.[2].

O she went out in a May morning,

In a May morning so gay,

But she never came back again,

Her auld father to see.

LADY ALICE

THE TEXT of this little ballad is given from Bell's *Ancient Poems, Ballads, and Songs of the Peasantry of England.*

It should be compared with *Lord Lovel.*

LADY ALICE

1.

1.[2] 'quoif,' cap. The line should doubtless be:— 'Mending her midnight quoif.'

LADY ALICE was sitting in her bower-window,

At midnight mending her quoif,

And there she saw as fine a corpse

As ever she saw in her life.

2.

'What bear ye, what bear ye, ye six men tall?

What bear ye on your shoulders?'

'We bear the corpse of Giles Collins,

An old and true lover of yours.'

3.

'O lay him down gently, ye six men tall,

All on the grass so green,

And to-morrow, when the sun goes down,

Lady Alice a corpse shall be seen.

4.

'And bury me in Saint Mary's church,

All for my love so true,

And make me a garland of marjoram,

And of lemon-thyme, and rue.'

5.

Giles Collins was buried all in the east,

Lady Alice all in the west,

And the roses that grew on Giles Collins's grave,

They reached Lady Alice's breast.

6.

The priest of the parish he chanced to pass,

And he severed those roses in twain;

Sure never were seen such true lovers before,

Nor e'er will there be again.

CHILD MAURICE

THE TEXT is from the Percy Folio, given *literatim*, with two rearrangements of the lines (in stt. 4 and 22) and a few obvious corrections, as suggested by Hales, and Furnivall, and Child. The Folio version was printed by Jamieson in his *Popular Ballads and Songs*.

The Scotch version, *Gil Morrice*, was printed by Percy in the *Reliques* in preference to the version of his Folio. He notes that the ballad 'has lately run through two editions in Scotland: the second was printed at Glasgow in 1755.' Thanks to an advertisement prefixed to these Scottish editions, sixteen additional verses were obtained and added by Percy, who thought that they were 'perhaps after all only an ingenious interpolation.' *Gil Morrice* introduces 'Lord Barnard' in place of 'John Steward,' adopted, perhaps, from *Little Musgrave and Lady Barnard*. Motherwell's versions were variously called *Child Noryce*, *Bob Norice*, *Gill Morice*, *Chield Morice*. Certainly the Folio ballad is unsurpassed for its vigorous, objective style, and forcible, vivid pictures.

THE STORY of this ballad gave rise to Home's *Douglas*, a tragedy, produced in the Concert Hall, Canongate, Edinburgh, 1756 (on which occasion the heroine's name was given as 'Lady Barnard'), and transferred to Covent Garden Theatre, in London, in 1757, the heroine's name being altered to 'Lady Randolph.'

Perhaps in the same year in which the play was produced in London, the poet Gray wrote from Cambridge:— 'I have got the old Scotch ballad on which *Douglas* was founded; it is divine, and as long as from hence to Aston. Aristotle's best rules are observed in it in a manner which shows the author never had heard of Aristotle. It begins in the fifth act of the play. You may read it two-thirds through without guessing what it is about; and yet, when you come to the end, it is impossible not to understand the whole story.'

CHILD MAURICE

    1.

    1.[1] 'siluer': the Folio gives *siluen*.

    CHILD MAURICE hunted ithe siluer wood,

    He hunted itt round about,

And noebodye that he ffound therin,

Nor none there was with-out.

2.

. . . . .

. . . . .

And he tooke his siluer combe in his hand,

To kembe his yellow lockes.

3.

He sayes, 'Come hither, thou litle ffoot-page,

That runneth lowlye by my knee,

Ffor thou shalt goe to Iohn Stewards wiffe

And pray her speake with mee.

4.

4.[3,4] These lines in the Folio precede st. 6.

. . . . .

. . . . .

I, and greete thou doe that ladye well,

Euer soe well ffroe mee.

5.

5.[2] *i.e.* as many times as there are knots knit in a net for the hair; cf. French *cale*.

5.[3] 'leeue,' lovely.

'And, as itt ffalls, as many times

As knotts beene knitt on a kell,

Or marchant men gone to leeue London

Either to buy ware or sell;

6.

'And, as itt ffalles, as many times

As any hart can thinke,

Or schoole-masters are in any schoole-house

Writting with pen and inke:

Ffor if I might, as well as shee may,

This night I wold with her speake.

7.

'And heere I send her a mantle of greene,

As greene as any grasse,

And bid her come to the siluer wood,

To hunt with Child Maurice.

8.

8.4 'Let,' fail: it is the infinitive, governed by 'bidd.'

'And there I send her a ring of gold,

A ring of precyous stone,

And bidd her come to the siluer wood,

Let ffor no kind of man.'

9.

9.1 'yode,' went.

9.4 'blan,' lingered.

One while this litle boy he yode,

Another while he ran,

Vntill he came to Iohn Stewards hall,

I-wis he never blan.

10.

And of nurture the child had good,

Hee ran vp hall and bower ffree,

And when he came to this lady ffaire,

Sayes, 'God you saue and see!

11.

- 210 -

'I am come ffrom Child Maurice,

A message vnto thee;

And Child Maurice, he greetes you well,

And euer soe well ffrom mee;

12.

'And, as itt ffalls, as oftentimes

As knotts beene knitt on a kell,

Or marchant-men gone to leeue London

Either ffor to buy ware or sell;

13.

13.³ 'are': omitted in the Folio.

'And as oftentimes he greetes you well

As any hart can thinke,

Or schoolemasters are in any schoole,

Wryting with pen and inke.

14.

'And heere he sends a mantle of greene,

As greene as any grasse,

And he bidds you come to the siluer wood,

To hunt with Child Maurice.

15.

'And heere he sends you a ring of gold,

A ring of the precyous stone;

He prayes you to come to the siluer wood,

Let ffor no kind of man.'

16.

'Now peace, now peace, thou litle ffoot-page,

Ffor Christes sake, I pray thee!

Ffor if my lord heare one of these words,

Thou must be hanged hye!'

17.

Iohn Steward stood vnder the castle-wall,

And he wrote the words euerye one,

. . . . .
. . . . .

18.

18.[3] 'I,' aye.

And he called vnto his hors-keeper,

'Make readye you my steede!'

I, and soe he did to his chamberlaine,

'Make readye thou my weede!'

19.

19.[1] 'lease,' leash, thong, string: perhaps for bringing back any game he might kill.

And he cast a lease vpon his backe,

And he rode to the siluer wood,

And there he sought all about,

About the siluer wood.

20.

And there he ffound him Child Maurice

Sitting vpon a blocke,

With a siluer combe in his hand,

Kembing his yellow locke.

* * * * *

21.

After 20 at least one verse is lost.

But then stood vp him Child Maurice,

And sayd these words trulye:

'I doe not know your ladye,' he said,
'If that I doe her see.'

22.

22.[1,2] In the Folio these lines precede 21.[1,2].
He sayes, 'How now, how now, Child Maurice?
Alacke, how may this bee?
Ffor thou hast sent her loue-tokens,
More now then two or three;

23.

'Ffor thou hast sent her a mantle of greene,
As greene as any grasse,
And bade her come to the siluer woode
To hunt with Child Maurice.

24.

24.[1] 'hast' omitted in the Folio.
'And thou [hast] sent her a ring of gold,
A ring of precyous stone,
And bade her come to the siluer wood,
Let ffor noe kind of man.

25.

25.[2] 'tone,' the one (or other).
'And by my ffaith, now, Child Maurice,
The tone of vs shall dye!'
'Now be my troth,' sayd Child Maurice,
'And that shall not be I.'

26.

But hee pulled forth a bright browne sword,
And dryed itt on the grasse,

And soe ffast he smote att Iohn Steward,

I-wisse he neuer rest.

27.

Then hee pulled fforth his bright browne sword,

And dryed itt on his sleeue,

And the ffirst good stroke Iohn Stewart stroke,

Child Maurice head he did cleeue.

28.

And he pricked itt on his swords poynt,

Went singing there beside,

And he rode till he came to that ladye ffaire,

Wheras this ladye lyed.

29.

And sayes, 'Dost thou know Child Maurice head,

If that thou dost itt see?

And lap itt soft, and kisse itt oft,

For thou louedst him better than mee.'

30.

But when shee looked on Child Maurice head,

She neuer spake words but three:

'I neuer beare no child but one,

And you haue slaine him trulye.'

31.

Sayes, 'Wicked be my merrymen all,

I gaue meate, drinke, and clothe!

But cold they not haue holden me

When I was in all that wrath!

32.

'Ffor I haue slaine one of the curteousest knights

That euer bestrode a steed,

Soe haue I done one [of] the fairest ladyes

That euer ware womans weede!'

FAUSE FOOTRAGE

THE TEXT is from Alexander Fraser Tytler's Brown MS., which was also the source of Scott's version in the *Minstrelsy*. One line (31.[1]), closely resembling a line in Lady Wardlaw's forged ballad *Hardyknute*, caused Sir Walter to investigate strictly the authenticity of the ballad, but the evidence of Lady Douglas, that she had learned the ballad in her childhood, and could still repeat much of it, removed his doubts. It is, however, quite possible, as Professor Child points out, 'that Mrs. Brown may unconsciously have adopted this verse from the tiresome and affected *Hardyknute*, so much esteemed in her day.'

THE STORY.—In *The Complaynt of Scotlande* (1549) there is mentioned a tale 'how the King of Estmure Land married the King's daughter of Westmure Land,' and it has been suggested that there is a connection with the ballad.

This is another of the ballads of which the English form has become so far corrupted that we have to seek its Scandinavian counterpart to obtain the full form of the story. The ballad is especially popular in Denmark, where it is found in twenty-three manuscripts, as follows:—

The rich Svend wooes Lisbet, who favours William for his good qualities. Svend, ill with grief, is well-advised by his mother, not to care for a plighted maid, and ill-advised by his sister, to kill William. Svend takes the latter advice, and kills William. Forty weeks later, Lisbet gives birth to a son, but Svend is told that the child is a girl. Eighteen years later, the young William, sporting with a peasant, quarrels with him; the peasant retorts, 'You had better avenge your father's death.' Young William asks his mother who slew his father, and she, thinking him too young to fight, counsels him to bring Svend to a court. William charges him in the court with the murder of his father, and says that no compensation has been offered. Not a penny shall be paid, says Svend. William draws his sword, and slays him.

Icelandic, Swedish, and Färöe ballads tell a similar story.

FAUSE FOOTRAGE

1.

KING EASTER has courted her for her gowd,

King Wester for her fee;

King Honor for her lands sae braid,

And for her fair body.

2.

They had not been four months married,

As I have heard them tell,

Until the nobles of the land

Against them did rebel.

3.

3.[1] 'kaivles,' lots.

And they cast kaivles them amang,

And kaivles them between;

And they cast kaivles them amang,

Wha shoud gae kill the king.

4.

O some said yea, and some said nay,

Their words did not agree;

Till up it gat him Fa'se Footrage,

And sware it shoud be he.

5.

When bells were rung, and mass was sung,

And a' man boon to bed,

King Honor and his gay ladie

In a hie chamer were laid.

6.

Then up it raise him Fa'se Footrage,

While a' were fast asleep,

And slew the porter in his lodge,

That watch and ward did keep.

7.

O four and twenty silver keys

Hang hie upon a pin,

And ay as a door he did unlock,

He has fasten'd it him behind.

8.

Then up it raise him King Honor,

Says, 'What means a' this din?

Now what's the matter, Fa'se Footrage,

Or wha was't loot you in?'

9.

'O ye my errand well shall learn

Before that I depart';

Then drew a knife baith lang and sharp

And pierced him thro' the heart.

10.

Then up it got the Queen hersell,

And fell low down on her knee:

'O spare my life now, Fa'se Footrage!

For I never injured thee.

11.

'O spare my life now, Fa'se Footrage!

Until I lighter be!

And see gin it be lad or lass,

King Honor has left me wi'.'

12.

'O gin it be a lass,' he says,

'Weel nursed she shall be;

But gin it be a lad-bairn,

He shall be hanged hie.

13.

13.⁴ 'gallows-pin,' the projecting beam of the gallows.

'I winna spare his tender age,
Nor yet his hie, hie kin;
But as soon as e'er he born is,
He shall mount the gallows-pin.'

14.

O four and twenty valiant knights
Were set the Queen to guard,
And four stood ay at her bower-door,
To keep baith watch and ward.

15.

But when the time drew till an end
That she should lighter be,
She cast about to find a wile
To set her body free.

16.

16.¹ 'birled,' plied.

16.⁴ 'wallwood,' wild wood: a conventional ballad-phrase.

O she has birled these merry young men
Wi' strong beer and wi' wine,
Until she made them a' as drunk
As any wall-wood swine.

17.

'O narrow, narrow is this window,
And big, big am I grown!'
Yet thro' the might of Our Ladie,
Out at it she has won.

18.

She wander'd up, she wander'd down,
She wander'd out and in;
And at last, into the very swines' stye,
The Queen brought forth a son.

19.

Then they cast kaivles them amang
Wha should gae seek the Queen;
And the kaivle fell upon Wise William,
And he's sent his wife for him.

20.

O when she saw Wise William's wife,
The Queen fell on her knee;
'Win up, win up, madame,' she says,
'What means this courtesie?'

21.

'O out of this I winna rise,
Till a boon ye grant to me,
To change your lass for this lad-bairn,
King Honor left me wi'.

22.

'And ye maun learn my gay gos-hawke
Well how to breast a steed;
And I shall learn your turtle-dow
As well to write and read.

23.

'And ye maun learn my gay gos-hawke
To wield baith bow and brand;
And I sall learn your turtle-dow

To lay gowd wi' her hand.

24.

'At kirk and market where we meet,
We dare nae mair avow
But—"Dame, how does my gay gose-hawk?"
"Madame, how does my dow?"'

25.

25.² A stock ballad-phrase.

When days were gane, and years come on,
Wise William he thought long;
Out has he ta'en King Honor's son,
A hunting for to gang.

26.

It sae fell out at their hunting,
Upon a summer's day,
That they cam' by a fair castle,
Stood on a sunny brae.

27.

'O dinna ye see that bonny castle
Wi' wa's and towers sae fair?
Gin ilka man had back his ain,
Of it you shoud be heir.'

28.

'How I shoud be heir of that castle,
In sooth I canna see;
When it belongs to Fa'se Footrage,
And he's nae kin to me.'

29.

'O gin ye shoud kill him Fa'se Footrage,
You woud do what is right;
For I wot he kill'd your father dear,
Ere ever you saw the light.
30.
'Gin you shoud kill him Fa'se Footrage,
There is nae man durst you blame;
For he keeps your mother a prisoner,
And she dares no take you hame.'

31.
The boy stared wild like a gray gose-hawk,
Says, 'What may a' this mean?'
'My boy, you are King Honor's son,
And your mother's our lawful queen.'
32.
'O gin I be King Honor's son,
By Our Ladie I swear,
This day I will that traytour slay,
And relieve my mother dear!'
33.
33.[1] A ballad conventionality.
He has set his bent bow till his breast,
And lap the castle-wa';
And soon he's siesed on Fa'se Footrage,
Wha loud for help gan ca'.
34.
'O haud your tongue now, Fa'se Footrage,
Frae me ye shanno flee.'

Syne pierced him through the foul fa'se heart,
And set his mother free.

35.

And he has rewarded Wise William
Wi' the best half of his land;
And sae has he the turtle dow
Wi' the truth o' his right hand.

FAIR ANNIE OF ROUGH ROYAL

'Ouvre ta port', Germin', c'est moi qu'est ton mari.'

'Donnez-moi des indic's de la première nuit,

Et par là je croirai que vous et's mon mari.'

—*Germaine.*

THE TEXT is Fraser Tytler's, taken down from the recitation of Mrs. Brown in 1800, who had previously (1783) recited a similar version to Jamieson. The later recitation, which was used by Scott, with others, seems to contain certain improvisations of Mrs. Brown's which do not appear in the earlier form.

THE STORY.—A mother, who feigns to be her own son and demands tokens of the girl outside the gate, turns her son's love away, and is cursed by him. Similar ballads exist in France, Germany, and Greece.

There is an early eighteenth-century MS. (Elizabeth Cochrane's *Song-Book*) of this ballad, which gives a preliminary history. Isabel of Rochroyal dreams of her love Gregory; she rises up, calls for a swift steed, and rides forth till she meets a company. They ask her who she is, and are told that she is 'Fair Isabel of Rochroyal,' seeking her true-love Gregory. They direct her to 'yon castle'; and thenceforth the tale proceeds much as in the other versions.

'Lochryan,' says Scott, 'lies in Galloway. Roch—or Rough—royal, I have not found, but there is a Rough castle in Stirlingshire' (Child).

FAIR ANNIE OF ROUGH ROYAL

1.

'O WHA will shoe my fu' fair foot?

And wha will glove my hand?

And wha will lace my middle jimp,

Wi' the new-made London band?

2.

'And wha will kaim my yellow hair,

Wi' the new-made silver kaim?

And wha will father my young son,

Till Love Gregor come hame?'

3.

'Your father will shoe your fu' fair foot,

Your mother will glove your hand;

Your sister will lace your middle jimp

Wi' the new-made London band.

4.

'Your brother will kaim your yellow hair,

Wi' the new-made silver kaim;

And the king of heaven will father your bairn,

Till Love Gregor come haim.'

5.

'But I will get a bonny boat,

And I will sail the sea,

For I maun gang to Love Gregor,

Since he canno come hame to me.'

6.

O she has gotten a bonny boat,

And sail'd the sa't sea fame;

She lang'd to see her ain true-love,

Since he could no come hame.

7.

'O row your boat, my mariners,

And bring me to the land,

For yonder I see my love's castle,

Closs by the sa't sea strand.'

8.

She has ta'en her young son in her arms,

And to the door she's gone,

And lang she's knock'd and sair she ca'd,

But answer got she none.

9.

'O open the door, Love Gregor,' she says,

'O open, and let me in;

For the wind blaws thro' my yellow hair,

And the rain draps o'er my chin.'

10.

10.[3] 'warlock,' wizard, magician.

'Awa', awa', ye ill woman,

You 'r nae come here for good;

You 'r but some witch, or wile warlock,

Or mer-maid of the flood.'

11.

'I am neither a witch nor a wile warlock,

Nor mer-maid of the sea,

I am Fair Annie of Rough Royal;

O open the door to me.'

12.

'Gin ye be Annie of Rough Royal—

And I trust ye are not she—

Now tell me some of the love-tokens

That past between you and me.'

13.

'O dinna you mind now, Love Gregor,

When we sat at the wine,

How we changed the rings frae our fingers?

And I can show thee thine.

14.

'O yours was good, and good enneugh,

But ay the best was mine;

For yours was o' the good red goud,

But mine o' the dimonds fine.

15.

'But open the door now, Love Gregor,

O open the door I pray,

For your young son that is in my arms

Will be dead ere it be day.'

16.

'Awa', awa', ye ill woman,

For here ye shanno win in;

Gae drown ye in the raging sea,

Or hang on the gallows-pin.'

17.

When the cock had crawn, and day did dawn,

And the sun began to peep,

Then it raise him Love Gregor,

And sair, sair did he weep.

18.

18.² 'gars me greet,' makes me weep.

'O I dream'd a dream, my mother dear,

The thoughts o' it gars me greet,

That Fair Annie of Rough Royal

Lay cauld dead at my feet.'

19.

'Gin it be for Annie of Rough Royal
That ye make a' this din,
She stood a' last night at this door,
But I trow she wan no in.'

20.
'O wae betide ye, ill woman,
An ill dead may ye die!
That ye woudno open the door to her,
Nor yet woud waken me.'
21.
O he has gone down to yon shore-side,
As fast as he could fare;
He saw Fair Annie in her boat
But the wind it toss'd her sair.
22.
And 'Hey, Annie!' and 'How, Annie!
O Annie, winna ye bide?'
But ay the mair that he cried 'Annie,'
The braider grew the tide.
23.
And 'Hey, Annie!' and 'How, Annie!
Dear Annie, speak to me!'
But ay the louder he cried 'Annie,'
The louder roar'd the sea.
24.
The wind blew loud, the sea grew rough,
And dash'd the boat on shore;
Fair Annie floats on the raging sea,

But her young son raise no more.

25.

Love Gregor tare his yellow hair,
And made a heavy moan;
Fair Annie's corpse lay at his feet,
But his bonny young son was gone.

26.

O cherry, cherry was her cheek,
And gowden was her hair,
But clay cold were her rosey lips,
Nae spark of life was there.

27.

And first he's kiss'd her cherry cheek,
And neist he's kissed her chin;
And saftly press'd her rosey lips,
But there was nae breath within.

28.

'O wae betide my cruel mother,
And an ill dead may she die!
For she turn'd my true-love frae the door,
When she came sae far to me.'

HIND HORN

THE TEXT is from Motherwell's MS., written from the recitation of a Mrs. King of Kilbarchan.

THE STORY of the ballad is a mere remnant of the story told in the Gest of King Horn, preserved in three manuscripts, the oldest of which belongs to the thirteenth century. Similar stories are given in a French romance of the fourteenth century, and an English manuscript of the same date. The complete story in the Gest may be condensed as follows:—

Horn, son of Murry, King of Suddenne, was captured by Saracens, who killed his father, and turned him and his twelve companions adrift in a boat, which was eventually beached safely on the coast of Westerness, and Ailmar the king took them in and brought them up. Rymenhild his daughter, falling in love with Horn, offered herself to him. He refused, unless she would make the king knight him. She did so, and again claimed his love; but he said he must first prove his knighthood. She gave him a ring set with stones, such that he could never be slain if he looked on it and thought of her. His first feat was the slaying of a hundred heathens; then he returned to Rymenhild. Meanwhile, however, one of his companions had told the king that Horn meant to kill him and wed his daughter. Ailmar ordered Horn to quit his court; and Horn, having told Rymenhild that if he did not come back in seven years she might marry another, sailed to the court of King Thurston in Ireland, where he stayed for seven years, performing feats of valour with the aid of Rymenhild's ring.

At the end of the allotted time, Rymenhild was to be married to King Modi of Reynis. Horn, hearing of this, went back to Westerness, arrived on the marriage-morn, met a palmer (the old beggar man of the ballad), changed clothes with him, and entered the hall. According to custom, Rymenhild served wine to the guests, and as Horn drank, he dropped her ring into the vessel. When she discovered it, she sent for the palmer, and questioned him. He said Horn had died on the voyage thither. Rymenhild seized a knife she had hidden to kill King Modi and herself if Horn came not, and set it to her breast. The palmer threw off his disguise, saying, 'I am Horn.' Still he would not wed her till he had regained his father's kingdom of Suddenne, and went away and did so. Meanwhile a false friend seized Rymenhild; but on the marriage-day Horn returned, killed him, and finally made Rymenhild his wife and Queen of Suddenne.

Compare the story of Torello and the Saladin in the *Decameron*, Tenth Day, Novel 9.

HIND HORN

1.

IN Scotland there was a babie born,

Lill lal, etc.

And his name it was called young Hind Horn,

With a fal lal, etc.

2.

He sent a letter to our king

That he was in love with his daughter Jean.[B]

* * * * *

3.

[B] After stanza 2 there is a gap in the story. Other versions say that Hind Horn goes, or is sent, to sea.

He's gi'en to her a silver wand,

With seven living lavrocks sitting thereon.

4.

She's gi'en to him a diamond ring,

With seven bright diamonds set therein.

5.

'When this ring grows pale and wan,

You may know by it my love is gane.'

6.

One day as he looked his ring upon,

He saw the diamonds pale and wan.

7.

He left the sea and came to land,

And the first that he met was an old beggar man.

8.

'What news, what news?' said young Hind Horn;

'No news, no news,' said the old beggar man.

9.

'No news,' said the beggar, 'no news at a',

But there is a wedding in the king's ha'.

10.

10.² The bride has lingered six weeks in hopes of Hind Horn's return.

'But there is a wedding in the king's ha',

That has halden these forty days and twa.'

11.

'Will ye lend me your begging coat?

And I'll lend you my scarlet cloak.

12.

12.¹ 'rung,' staff.

'Will you lend me your beggar's rung?

And I'll gi'e you my steed to ride upon.

13.

'Will you lend me your wig o' hair,

To cover mine, because it is fair?'

14.

The auld beggar man was bound for the mill,

But young Hind Horn for the king's hall.

15.

The auld beggar man was bound for to ride,

But young Hind Horn was bound for the bride.

16.

When he came to the king's gate,

He sought a drink for Hind Horn's sake.

17.

The bride came down with a glass of wine,

When he drank out the glass, and dropt in the ring.

18.

'O got ye this by sea or land?

Or got ye it off a dead man's hand?'

19.

'I got not it by sea, I got it by land,

And I got it, madam, out of your own hand.'

20.

'O I'll cast off my gowns of brown,

And beg wi' you frae town to town.

21.

'O I'll cast off my gowns of red,

And I'll beg wi' you to win my bread.'

22.

'Ye needna cast off your gowns of brown,

For I'll make you lady o' many a town.

23.

'Ye needna cast off your gowns of red,

It's only a sham, the begging o' my bread.'

24.

The bridegroom he had wedded the bride,

But young Hind Horn he took her to bed.

EDWARD

THE TEXT is that given by Percy in the *Reliques* (1765), with the substitution of *w* for initial *qu*, and *y* for initial *ȝ*, as in *Young Waters* (see p. 146). In the fourth edition of the *Reliques* Percy states that 'this curious song was transmitted to the editor by Sir David Dalrymple, Bart., late Lord Hailes.'

Percy's adoption of antique spelling in this ballad has caused some doubt to be thrown on its authenticity; but there is also a version *Son Davie*, given in his *Minstrelsy* by Motherwell, who, in referring to the version in the *Reliques*, said there was reason for believing that Lord Hailes 'made a few slight verbal improvements in the copy he transmitted, and altered the hero's name to Edward, a name which, by the bye, never occurs in a Scottish ballad except where allusion is made to an English king.'

THE STORY has a close parallel in Swedish, the form of the ballad remaining in dialogue.

Motherwell points out that the verses of which *Edward* consists generally form the conclusion of the ballad of *The Twa Brothers*, and also of certain versions of *Lizie Wan*; and is inclined to regard *Edward* as detached from one of those ballads. More probably the reverse is the case, that the story of *Edward* has been attached to the other ballads.

The present version of the ballad exhibits an unusual amplification of the refrain. The story is told in two lines of each eight-lined stanza; but the lyrical effect added by the elaborate refrain is almost unique.

EDWARD

 1.

 'WHY dois your brand sae drap wi' bluid,

 Edward, Edward?

 Why dois your brand sae drap wi' bluid,

 And why sae sad gang yee, O?'

 'O, I hae killed my hauke sae guid,

 Mither, mither:

 O, I hae killed my hauke sae guid,

And I had nae mair bot hee, O.'

2.

'Your haukis bluid was nevir sae reid,

Edward, Edward.

Your haukis bluid was nevir sae reid,

My deir son I tell thee, O.'

'O, I hae killed my reid-roan steid,

Mither, mither:

O, I hae killed my reid-roan steid,

That erst was sae fair and frie, O.'

3.

3.4 'dule,' grief; 'drie,' suffer.

'Your steid was auld, and ye hae gat mair,

Edward, Edward:

Your steid was auld, and ye hae gat mair,

Sum other dule ye drie, O.'

'O, I hae killed my fadir deir,

Mither, mither:

O, I hae killed my fadir deir,

Alas! and wae is mee, O!'

4.

'And whatten penance wul ye drie for that,

Edward, Edward?

And whatten penance will ye drie for that,

My deir son, now tell me, O,

'Ile set my feit in yonder boat,

Mither, mither:

Ile set my feit in yonder boat,

- 235 -

And Ile fare ovir the sea, O.'

5.

'And what wul ye doe wi' your towirs and your ha',
Edward, Edward?
And what wul ye doe wi' your towirs and your ha',
That were sae fair to see, O?'
'Ile let thame stand tul they doun fa',
Mither, mither:
Ile let thame stand tul they doun fa',
For here nevir mair maun I bee, O.'

6.

6.[5,7] *i.e.* The world is wide.

'And what wul ye leive to your bairns and your wife,
Edward, Edward?
And what wul ye leive to your bairns and your wife,
Whan ye gang ovir the sea, O?'
'The warldis room, late them beg thrae life,
Mither, mither:
The warldis room, let them beg thrae life,
For thame nevir mair wul I see, O.'

7.

'And what wul ye leive to your ain mither deir,
Edward, Edward?
And what wul ye leive to your ain mither deir?
My deir son, now tell me, O.'
'The curse of hell frae me sall ye beir,
Mither, mither:
The curse of hell frae me sall ye beir,
Sic counseils ye gave to me, O.'

LORD RANDAL

THE TEXT is from Scott's *Minstrelsy of the Scottish Border* (1803). Other forms give the name as *Lord Ronald*, but Scott retains *Randal* on the supposition that the ballad originated in the death of 'Thomas Randolph, or Randal, Earl of Murray, nephew to Robert Bruce, and governor of Scotland,' who died at Musselburgh in 1332.

THE STORY of the ballad is found in Italian tradition nearly three hundred years ago, and also occurs in Dutch, German, Swedish, Danish, Magyar, Wendish, etc.

Certain variants of the ballad bear the title of *The Croodlin Doo*, and the 'handsome young man' is changed for a child, and the poisoner is the child's step-mother. Scott suggests that this change was made 'to excite greater interest in the nursery.' In nearly all forms of the ballad, the poisoning is done by the substitution of snakes ('eels') for fish, a common method amongst the ancients of administering poison.

Child gives a collation of seven versions secured in America of late years, in each of which the name of Lord Randal has become corrupted to 'Tiranti.'

The antiphonetic form of the ballad is popular, as being dramatic and suitable for singing. Compare *Edward*, also a dialogue between mother and son.

LORD RANDAL

1.

'O WHERE hae ye been, Lord Randal, my son?

O where hae ye been, my handsome young man?'

'I hae been to the wild wood; mother, make my bed soon,

For I'm weary wi' hunting, and fain wald lie down.'

2.

'Where gat ye your dinner, Lord Randal, my son?

Where gat ye your dinner, my handsome young man?'

'I din'd wi' my true-love; mother, make my bed soon,

For I'm weary wi' hunting, and fain wald lie down.'

3.

3.³ 'broo',' broth.

'What gat ye to your dinner, Lord Randal, my son?
What gat ye to your dinner, my handsome young man?'
'I gat eels boil'd in broo'; mother, make my bed soon,
For I'm weary wi' hunting, and fain wald lie down.'

4.

'What became of your bloodhounds, Lord Randal, my son?
What became of your bloodhounds, my handsome young man?'
'O they swell'd and they died; mother, make my bed soon,
For I'm weary wi' hunting, and fain wald lie down.'
5.
'O I fear ye are poison'd, Lord Randal, my son!
O I fear ye are poison'd, my handsome young man!'
'O yes, I am poison'd; mother, make my bed soon,
For I'm sick at the heart, and I fain wald lie down.'

LAMKIN

THE TEXT is from Jamieson's *Popular Ballads*. He obtained it from Mrs. Brown. It is by far the best version of a score or so in existence. The name of the hero varies from Lamkin, Lankin, Lonkin, etc., to Rankin and Balcanqual. I have been informed by Andrew McDowall, Esq., of an incomplete version in which Lamkin's name has become 'Bold Hang'em.'

Finlay (*Scottish Ballads*) remarks:— 'All reciters agree that Lammikin, or Lambkin, is not the name of the hero, but merely an epithet.'

THE STORY varies little throughout all the versions, though in some, as in one known to Percy, it lacks much of the detail here given.

LAMKIN

1.

IT's Lamkin was a mason good

As ever built wi' stane;

He built Lord Wearie's castle,

But payment got he nane.

2.

'O pay me, Lord Wearie,

Come, pay me my fee':

'I canna pay you, Lamkin,

For I maun gang o'er the sea.'

3.

'O pay me now, Lord Wearie,

Come, pay me out o' hand':

'I canna pay you, Lamkin,

Unless I sell my land.'

4.

'O gin ye winna pay me,

I here sail mak' a vow,

Before that ye come hame again,

Ye sall hae cause to rue.'

5.

Lord Wearie got a bonny ship,

To sail the saut sea faem;

Bade his lady weel the castle keep,

Ay till he should come hame.

6.

6.[1] 'limmer,' wretch, rascal.

But the nourice was a fause limmer

As e'er hung on a tree;

She laid a plot wi' Lamkin,

Whan her lord was o'er the sea.

7.

7.[3] 'shot-window': see special section of the Introduction.

She laid a plot wi' Lamkin,

When the servants were awa',

Loot him in at a little shot-window,

And brought him to the ha'.

8.

'O whare's a' the men o' this house,

That ca' me Lamkin?'

'They're at the barn-well thrashing;

'Twill be lang ere they come in.'

9.

'And whare's the women o' this house,

That ca' me Lamkin?'

'They're at the far well washing;

'Twill be lang ere they come in.'

10.

'And whare's the bairns o' this house,

That ca' me Lamkin?'

'They're at the school reading;

'Twill be night or they come hame.'

11.

'O whare's the lady o' this house,

That ca's me Lamkin?'

'She's up in her bower sewing,

But we soon can bring her down.'

12.

12.² 'gaire'; *i.e.* by his knee: see special section of the Introduction.

Then Lamkin's tane a sharp knife,

That hung down by his gaire,

And he has gi'en the bonny babe

A deep wound and a sair.

13.

13.³ 'bore,' hole, crevice.

Then Lamkin he rocked,

And the fause nourice sang,

Till frae ilkae bore o' the cradle

The red blood out sprang.

14.

14.⁴ 'greeting,' crying.

Then out it spak' the lady,

As she stood on the stair:

'What ails my bairn, nourice,

That he's greeting sae sair?

15.

'O still my bairn, nourice,

O still him wi' the pap!'

'He winna still, lady,

For this nor for that.'

16.

'O still my bairn, nourice,

O still him wi' the wand!'

'He winna still, lady,

For a' his father's land.'

17.

'O still my bairn, nourice,

O still him wi' the bell!'

'He winna still, lady,

Till ye come down yoursel'.'

18.

O the firsten step she steppit,

She steppit on a stane;

But the neisten step she steppit,

She met him Lamkin.

19.

'O mercy, mercy, Lamkin,

Hae mercy upon me!

Though you've ta'en my young son's life,

Ye may let mysel' be.'

20.

'O sall I kill her, nourice,

Or sall I lat her be?'
'O kill her, kill her, Lamkin,
For she ne'er was good to me.'
21.
'O scour the bason, nourice,
And mak' it fair and clean,
For to keep this lady's heart's blood,
For she's come o' noble kin.'

22.
'There need nae bason, Lamkin,
Lat it run through the floor;
What better is the heart's blood
O' the rich than o' the poor?'
23.
23.[3] 'dowie,' sad.
But ere three months were at an end,
Lord Wearie came again;
But dowie, dowie was his heart
When first he came hame.
24.
24.[2] 'chamer,' chamber.
24.[4] 'lamer,' amber.
'O wha's blood is this,' he says,
'That lies in the chamer?'
'It is your lady's heart's blood;
'T is as clear as the lamer.'
25.
25.[4] 'ava,' at all.

'And wha's blood is this,' he says,

'That lies in my ha'?'

'It is your young son's heart's blood;

'Tis the clearest ava.'

26.

26.³ 'grat,' greeted, wept.

O sweetly sang the black-bird

That sat upon the tree;

But sairer grat Lamkin,

When he was condemn'd to die.

27.

And bonny sang the mavis

Out o' the thorny brake;

But sairer grat the nourice,

When she was tied to the stake.

FAIR MARY OF WALLINGTON

THE TEXT is from *Lovely Jenny's Garland*, as given with emendations by Professor Child. There is also a curiously perverted version in Herd's manuscript, in which the verses require rearrangement before becoming intelligible.

THE STORY can be gathered from the version here given without much difficulty. It turns on the marriage of Fair Mary, who is one of seven sisters fated to die of their first child. Fair Mary seems to be a fatalist, and, after vowing never to marry, accepts as her destiny the hand of Sir William Fenwick of Wallington. Three-quarters of a year later she sends to fair Pudlington for her mother. Her mother is much affected at the news (st. 22), and goes to Wallington. Her daughter, in travail, lays the blame on her, cuts open her side to give birth to an heir, and dies.

In a Breton ballad Pontplancoat thrice marries a Marguerite, and each of his three sons costs his mother her life.

In the Scottish ballad, a 'scope' is put in Mary's mouth when the operation takes place. In the Breton ballad it is a silver spoon or a silver ball. 'Scope,' or 'scobs' as it appears in Herd, means a gag, and was apparently used to prevent her from crying out. But the silver spoon and ball in the Breton ballad would appear to have been used for Marguerite to bite on in her anguish, just as sailors chewed bullets while being flogged.

FAIR MARY OF WALLINGTON

1.

1.¹ 'silly,' simple.

1.⁴ 'lair,' lying-in.

WHEN we were silly sisters seven,

Sisters were so fair,

Five of us were brave knights' wives,

And died in childbed lair.

2.

2.⁴ 'gate,' way.

Up then spake Fair Mary,

Marry woud she nane;

If ever she came in man's bed,

The same gate wad she gang.

3.

'Make no vows, Fair Mary,

For fear they broken be;

Here's been the Knight of Wallington,

Asking good will of thee.'

4.

'If here's been the knight, mother,

Asking good will of me,

Within three quarters of a year

You may come bury me.'

5.

5.[3] 'her mother' is, of course, her mother-in-law.

When she came to Wallington,

And into Wallington hall,

There she spy'd her mother dear,

Walking about the wall.

6.

'You're welcome, daughter dear,

To thy castle and thy bowers';

'I thank you kindly, mother,

I hope they'll soon be yours.'

7.

She had not been in Wallington

Three quarters and a day,

Till upon the ground she could not walk,

She was a weary prey.

8.

She had not been in Wallington
Three quarters and a night,
Till on the ground she coud not walk,
She was a weary wight.

9.

9.² 'shun' = shoon, shoes.

'Is there ne'er a boy in this town,
Who'll win hose and shun,
That will run to fair Pudlington,
And bid my mother come?'

10.

Up then spake a little boy,
Near unto a-kin;
'Full oft I have your errands gone,
But now I will it run.'

11.

Then she call'd her waiting-maid
To bring up bread and wine;
'Eat and drink, my bonny boy,
Thou'll ne'er eat more of mine.

12.

'Give my respects to my mother,
She sits in her chair of stone,
And ask her how she likes the news,
Of seven to have but one.

13.

13. This stanza is not in the original, but is supplied from the boy's repetition, st. 19.

13.⁴ 'lake-wake' = lyke-wake: watching by a corpse.

'Give my respects to my mother,

As she sits in her chair of oak,

And bid her come to my sickening,

Or my merry lake-wake.

14.

'Give my love to my brother

William, Ralph, and John,

And to my sister Betty fair,

And to her white as bone:

15.

'And bid her keep her maidenhead,

Be sure make much on 't,

For if e'er she come in man's bed,

The same gate will she gang.'

16.

Away this little boy is gone,

As fast as he could run;

When he came where brigs were broke,

He lay down and swum.

17.

When he saw the lady, he said,

'Lord may your keeper be!'

'What news, my pretty boy,

Hast thou to tell to me?'

18.

'Your daughter Mary orders me,

As you sit in a chair of stone,

To ask you how you like the news,

Of seven to have but one.

19.

'Your daughter gives commands,

As you sit in a chair of oak,

And bids you come to her sickening,

Or her merry lake-wake.

20.

'She gives command to her brother

William, Ralph, and John,

[And] to her sister Betty fair,

And to her white as bone.

21.

'She bids her keep her maidenhead,

Be sure make much on 't,

For if e'er she came in man's bed,

The same gate woud she gang.'

22.

22. This, in ballads, is a customary method of giving expression to strong emotion.

She kickt the table with her foot,

She kickt it with her knee,

The silver plate into the fire,

So far she made it flee.

23.

Then she call'd her waiting-maid

To bring her riding-hood,

So did she on her stable-groom

To bring her riding-steed.

24.

'Go saddle to me the black, [the black,]

Go saddle to me the brown,

Go saddle to me the swiftest steed

That e'er rid [to] Wallington.'

25.

When they came to Wallington,

And into Wallington hall,

There she spy'd her son Fenwick,

Walking about the wall.

26.

'God save you, dear son,

Lord may your keeper be!

Where is my daughter fair,

That used to walk with thee?'

27.

He turn'd his head round about,

The tears did fill his e'e:

"'Tis a month' he said, 'since she

Took her chambers from me.'

28.

She went on   .   .   .

And there were in the hall

Four and twenty ladies,

Letting the tears down fall.

29.

29.[1] 'scope,' a gag.

Her daughter had a scope

Into her cheek and into her chin,

All to keep her life

Till her dear mother came.

30.

30.[4] 'wite,' blame: *i.e.* her mother was the cause of all her trouble.

'Come take the rings off my fingers,

The skin it is so white,

And give them to my mother dear,

For she was all the wite.

31.

'Come take the rings off my fingers,

The veins they are so red,

Give them to Sir William Fenwick,

I'm sure his heart will bleed.'

32.

She took out a razor

That was both sharp and fine,

And out of her left side has taken

The heir of Wallington.

33.

There is a race in Wallington,

And that I rue full sare;

Tho' the cradle it be full spread up

The bride-bed is left bare.